COLLECTED POEMS
1929–1974

JAMES REEVES

Collected Poems
1929-1974

HEINEMANN
LONDON

Heinemann Educational Books Ltd
LONDON   EDINBURGH   MELBOURNE
AUCKLAND   TORONTO   HONG KONG
SINGAPORE   KUALA LUMPUR   IBADAN
NAIROBI   JOHANNESBURG   NEW DELHI

ISBN 0 435 14770 6
ISBN 0 435 14771 4 (*limited edition*)

Published by
Heinemann Educational Books Ltd
48 Charles Street, London W1X 8AH
Printed in Great Britain by
Butler & Tanner Ltd, Frome and London

Contents

viii

In memory of
Mary Reeves 1910-1966

Note on the Poems

The 1960 edition of my *Collected Poems* has for some years been out of print. In this new edition I have included all the poems I want to reprint, both from the earlier collection and from the three small books published since 1960. I have reverted to a chronological order. Increasing distance from my earlier poems has made it possible for me to look at them objectively and to make a number of revisions. I have also added two previously uncollected poems.

The Natural Need
1936

HARTLAND QUAY

Go to the sea, then. Pack a bag and stay
Long enough to know the times of posts
And where to bathe and when, and to get brown.
Go and climb the inland-tilted cliffs
And scale the rocks that overhang the sea.
Pursue the glittering snailtrack over lichen
On hands and feet, and from the stony face
Chip crystals with the ferrule of your stick.

You'll turn your back on the indifferent sea,
View it no longer, let your ears reject
The gulls' falsetto, siren to your aim,
Leave spongy coombs and shallow rockpools, paths
That tempt you up to crests of gaudy ling,
Forget the cry of sunlight and salt wind,
The fragile bones of seabirds on the cliff
Forget such things, and since your blood responds
To the incessant wheedling of the sea,
Forget it too. Leave it for those not made
To stand in danger from its sorceries.

You are safer travelling homewards in a train,
Reading the paper, meeting other people
And eyes of friends, hurtful but undeceiving.
Deny the sea, the flattery of birds,
And starve corrupting elements from your blood.

SIRVENTES

Morning comes on five bells in a city of the Midi,
Wakens one troubled with dreams,
The man none trusted filches sleep from the gutter.
'Friend, we live in stirring times,
One day knows not the next.
My neighbour, late from whoring, fell at the spear's
    end.
Raimbaut the juggler, courting the Duchess,
Was stabbed on her threshold,
The Duke taken:
His horse reared, wood-smoke in the nostrils.'
'They that beset us
Some say fought for the priests,
Others for plunder.'
Here two slept in a curtained fastness,
Tumbled among tapestries and strewn silks,
Deaf to the banquet fled in confusion.

Lady, your eyes more bright than day
Behold, after the sword, the measure of decline,
Flames outstripping the scythe, and after these
Corruption.
A year of want is a year of questioning.
Was that my last song, spilt among wine-cups?
Shall tomorrow change cloister for palace?
Shall I praise a dry rod bearing fruit,
Remembering you are white and your teeth white,
You speak truth?
Shall I be heard to say,
Remembering the eight candles placed in the sepulchre
For Bertran de Born,

4

'We live, suffered not suffering,
To die in our beds?'
Kisses are on the forehead, after death.
We, having outlived torment, are yet unfulfilled,
Finding solace
In empty pain at midnight.

'Sirventes' was a form of Provençal poem, a conventional vehicle for satire. The first part of this poem is about the overthrow of a Provençal town during the Albigensian Wars of the early XIII century, the period of the decadence of Troubadour poetry. The Albigensian Crusade was promoted by the Pope in order to suppress the heresy and irreligion of the Courts, which patronised the poets, and was joined by genuine religious fanatics and by mercenary adventurers indiscriminately. The second part is a supposed address to his mistress by a Provençal poet of the end of this period. He is regretting the passing of a vigorous and pagan existence, its replacement by defeatist religious experience. He refers to the course taken by many of the poets after the Courts had been disbanded—that of going into monasteries, where the 'profane' love of classical Provençal poetry became the 'sacred' love of the Virgin. 'A dry Rod bearing fruit' is from a poem by Peire de Corbiac addressed to the Virgin ('verga seca frug fazens'). 'Your teeth white. You speak truth' is from a poem by Arnaut de Mareuil ('Blancas dens ab motz verais'). Bertran de Born, a poet of this period, ended his life as a monk. The only notice of his death (1215) is 'octava candela in sepulcro ponitur pro Bernardo de Born: cera tres solidos empta est'.

REPOSE

Repose is in simplicities.
Perhaps the mind has leaves like trees,
Luxuriant in the sensual sun
And tossed by wind's intricacies,
And finds repose is more than grief
When failing light and falling leaf
Denote that winter has begun.

AT THE WINDOW

Then more-than-morning quiet
The pretty lawn extended;
And rooted trees stood tall
On westward shadows pointing.

Answering no will, my hand
Dropped from the window catch,
My throat was undecided
Whether to sob or sing.

Why trees were not, nor morning,
No flash of mind revealed,
But throat and hands had greeted
A memory more clear than sight.

CLIMBING A MOUNTAIN

'Addío! Addío!' The guide and the guide's wife
Tenderly, in the warm hut before dawn,
Parted after the breakfast by lamplight;
And I went on, down the little path over the stream;
The guide came with the rope and the other things
And led the way up silently between the fir-trees.

Up and up, on dogged metal my feet carried me,
Towards the distant shoulder; above it hung
The watery and foreboding moon, fading.
In my eyes was the grey light
And the guide pointing to signs of the war,
Brutal, jagged wire and tumble-down dugouts:
In my heart—but I did not know where my heart was,
Or why the rocks above me seemed more brutal
Or my feet glad, carrying me up, out of the valley.

Dawn was above us, creeping down the white summit,
But we still were in twilight. I heard,
Under the scrunch of my feet across the gravel,
The stream's quick broken tumbling in the valley.
At last we reached the snow, and stopped. It was very
        lonely.
The guide undid his rucksack, saying something gay,
And we rigged ourselves out for crossing the snowfield.

I felt good in my legs, all dressed up like a Russian;
But my heart hadn't come with me—I knew that
        now,
Panting and stumbling. I had no competence,
I felt feeble and small after a while
As I struggled up behind the mountaineer.
We had to keep stopping, I was so weary.
A little wind would blow over the desolate snowfield
And the guide would breathe it; it was his breath.
When we came to rock again, it was the same:
He would look between rocks, down, down
Into the stony heart of the mountain,
And that would be his heart and the mountain-sides
        his sides.

When the wind dropped on the snowfield I would
        hear
The little stream bumping away in the valley,
And that would be my heart, I thought.
'Must you drone there always,' I said, 'will-less and
        idle?
Come up and help me, skulker in the depth!
My legs are faint now, my blood is without ambition.'
And my heart mumbled and became inaudible.

'Very well,' I thought, 'I will go without you.'
And on we went; we kicked our way out of the snow
And began to ascend over the rock. By this time
The dawn had been swallowed up in a moist haze.
Soon I was quite without pride, and the climber's
        emulation.
I let the guide haul me up over the difficult bits;
I didn't care what he thought of me,
I didn't want to get to the top—
Except that it was probably the quickest way down
        now.

I was glad when I stumbled off the rock
And stood on the edge of the snow plateau.
The guide looked at the snow and back at the rock
And he loved them both with his eyes,
Like a child caressing its own innocent flesh.
Then, as we went on across the last level,
There seemed nothing to breathe; I was unconscious;
And there was nothing to see either, except the snow
Sodden with mist, and yielding; leprous it seemed.

8

At the summit there was a book in a metal box.
We sat down and wrote in it solemnly.
I didn't look at the guide. I looked round me into the
    mist.
We took out our food. He gave me some red wine
    from his flask.
As he did so the flask clinked on the cup,
Hollow and dead in the rare muffled quiet.
At last he spoke, slowly, in his soft clinging tongue—
A sort of congratulation, and something sad about the
    weather.
Well, this was the top. In a way I was proud,
Though I'd nothing to be proud of, a failure in
    achievement.
I had lost my self, my heart, where the guide had
    found his.
My heart was down there all the time.
Perhaps now in the albergo, singing songs and
    drinking,
And laughing at the Italian tourists (the little heads
    and the big chests) .
Who buccaneered through their stolen country in
    shiny cars,
And the German tourists who came to gather plants.

But wasn't it good, my heart, to leave you for a
    while?
Wasn't it good, for a few hours, to wrench myself
Out of the sun's embrace, the indolent valley,
To spurn you, to be alone, to be comfortless?
Yes, churlish heart, it was good: to be lost
These long stolen hours from you—
First and most fulsome of counsellors.

GHOSTS AND PERSONS

Surely, though old,
This is not a ghosts' county,
No place of memory but simpler,
Where you forget a gradual spring
In summer's ready bounty.
Surely this is no ghosts' county.
In the pasture, open and green,
And on the downs, bare or tree-crested,
Can lurk nothing but the weasel and rabbit;
The nettle patch where the robins have nested
In a discarded soup-tureen
Can harbour none to rise and hail me
Boldly through my urban habit.
At dusk I know that the white presence
By the hedge is only cherry-blossom
And that the rustling in the copse
Is made by wakeful mice or pheasants.

Reassuring and free from guile
Are the farm-hands' good evening smile,
My ex-policeman neighbour's nod,
Marchment the gardener's Yes or No sir
Over his spade, and the request for orders
From an itinerant village grocer;
They see no stranger over my shoulder.
The thatcher at The Nag swilling his hire
And Mrs Farmer with her soft voice
And slow movements lighting the fire
Address me without suspicion
As a person and not an apparition.

Perhaps here I shall be
The self unhaunted whom they greet
And not meet
At this or that corner
The long or lately dead,
Me or a friend or a historical figure.
Perhaps, walking on the Roman road,
Noting the churns at farm-gates
And the blackthorn hedges, I shall say
'This is an innocent and new today
With no future but tomorrow's porridge.
This is me walking here and not the ghost
Of some legionary on the forage.'

Mrs Farmer's brother-in-law
Sold me the cottage—
To have which makes me feel
As if at length I am real
And not a visitant on another's freehold.
His mind's alleys are
With intricate superstitions keyholed.
But not all his lore and his herb-skill
Saved his wife from falling ill,
And all the horse-shoes over the doors,
Each with its original nails,
Could not keep death away.
Whereon by the clear light of dismay
He put up his house for sale.
And when the agent and the lawyer
Had finished crackling documents
And the brisk surveyor
Gathered his tackle and decamped
I thought, 'This is no ghost' estate.

Between the four walls and the slate,
Between the well and the big gate,
None but me has title here,
None but people shall appear
Because it is no ghosts' estate.'

Fifty years ago and more
My house was the village school.
But this I face with fortitude,
Feeling no tags of rhyme or rule
Strayed from copybook and primer
Can rise up to admonish me;
Nor in the evening from the spaces
The lamplight hollows in the gloom
Of the old schoolroom
Shall start the rudimentary faces
Of school children to astonish me,
The forward smile and stupid eyes
Of a youthful village charmer,
The dazed incomprehension of
The boy that became Mr Farmer,
Or slow heads drowsing over sums
While the afternoon creeps round
And the mower's distant sound
Through the high window comes.

From such memories may I be free
So that here I shall be
The self unhaunted who
Of many selves chose this place
And gave those selves the slip.
Such visions, horseshoes, keep from my door
And bring good luck now
If you never did before,

That night be not a meeting
Of old familiars
Nor cock-crow more a hallowed rite
Than a friendly greeting.

WINTER SPECULATION

We have travelled to a new country,
A region of hills
Where the sky is a frosted glass
Splintered with branches.
Winter piles up against the window ledges;
In our hearts the drifts deepen.
We are in a new country
And estranged.

Were you to die here,
Being delicate—
Were you to die after a season
And winter to surrender the hilltops finally,
Would not the whiteness melt from our hearts
And the river break
And I be left
Alone in the sunlight of a new country?

Here they tell me
Winter is long
Almost to forgetting spring.

THOUGHTS AND MEMORIES

Do others waking in the morning hear
Dog bark or cuckoo call
And suddenly not know for certain whether
Dog or bird was there at all?
Perhaps a poacher or a country boy
Is never taken unawares
But active with his snares
Is not so caught up in the past as I.

Do you too wonder if the finest thing
A promising flower can do
Is but to imitate with all its art
All other flowers that ever grew?
You looking from your window see the spring
Each year perform its leisurely
Long act of memory,
All nature gone into remembering.

Do you too lying sleepless think of things
That you have said or done,
Communicate with ghosts and fantasies
As if you feared to be alone?
You start to fall asleep, and one by one
Thoughts and memories go their ways;
You sleep and no ghost stays—
And oh, the horror if you waken then!

The Imprisoned Sea
1949

THE DANCERS

Too late he saw the watcher in the shade
Signal from the laurels beside the lawn,
The circle close and the loved figure vanish
In a maze of pointed feet, a flash of hair.
He heard the leaves of the sycamore complain.

Now to the garden the lapsed years recall
No cloaked betrayer and no mythical dancers
Who steal by moonlight in the month of August.
Instead, upon the lawn together pace
A child's ghost and a man of ageing heart.

TO A CHILD AT CHRISTMAS

I see your eyes like nightingales
Entangled in the spicy boughs,
So bright and dark they glow and sing
Amidst the multi-coloured stars
Where your desire from this night on
Shall find a bleak, inhospitable home.

Your thoughts explore the anguished night
Where treble voices carolling
Repeat the yet unanswered wish
In hope to melt a frozen world.
Slave to such music now, your heart
Will be for ever only half your own.

THE RIVER'S TROUBLE

The waters gather for the last descent
Through the intricate city to the sea,
Sliding past towers where the feet of queens went,
To the breweries and wharves and the laggard
    merchant hulls.
I hear the waters of the river say,
'We forget nothing, we remember the pebbly hills,
Not long ago we heard the sibillant reeds,
Tomorrow the city clocks and the harsh notes of
    gulls.'

But here the glass-grey reaches bear along
The heedless daughters of the world, the errant sons,
And here the snatching, serpent-headed swans
Ignore the parasols and banal songs,
Bending inviolable necks for buns.

Between the banks where the anglers ruminate
I note the voice of the unreturning waters,
'Our memory is a queen's ghost pacing slow
In the shadow of Arthurian walls amid the sedges
Where cygnets hatch and fish breed under the lilies.
Our memory is with us, troubling both day and
    night.
It will be with us as we lapse insensibly seaward
Attended by steam-barges and intimate canoes
With a wake of feline laughter, shreds of song,
And spittle aimed by barefoot boys on the bridges.

A queen's ghost moves with the abstracted gait
Of one recalling a forgotten purpose.
Even then it will trouble us as we thread the city,
Slipping beside the quay where rat-faced men scurry
Under the shadow of gas-holders and rattling cranes.
It will haunt us in the music of seagulls
And in the image of a yacht on the estuary.'

So rumoured the waters of the changeless river
Here in these middle reaches where for ever
The spoilt girls and their urgent squires consort.
Here is a spell laid, and all ignore
The river's voice—unless perhaps the swans
Hold in their memory what none would guess.

At a low inn with bowling-green beside
Where shirt-sleeved men at sundown stoop and aim,
The licensee, ex-royal servant, ponders,
Reckoning the empties, his vanished splendours,
Presented chairs of legendary worth,
The prince's indiscretions and so forth—
So too the swans may secretly revolve
The ruin of their times, and for a while
The undiscriminating sun may solve
Conflicts of squalor, vanity and greed.

FACES

The negro's face amidst the coke,
The giant's profile in the oak,
Are obliterated both
This by fire and that by growth.
Yet though it may be hours or years
That pass before the picture blurs
And though the awe is left behind
   That such things caused in childish days,
   An indefinable malaise
Remains to vex the adult mind.

THE CONSPIRATORS
1940

'Talk of the green time and birds on branches'
Said the ragged robin to the lords and ladies.
'Read him the tale of love ever after,'
The blackbird whistled in the summer wind.

'Your kind attention, your smooth enticements
Are vain distractions,' the listener said.
'Your knee-high grasses, your cavernous hedgerows,
Are secret as treason but they cannot hide

The man in blue lying deep in the ditch,
His eyes gaping, his limbs askew,
And out of his nonchalant mouth a trickle
Red and crooked as the rivers of Hell.'

BESTIARY

Happy the quick-eyed lizard that pursues
    Its creviced zigzag race
Amid the epic ruins of a temple
    Leaving no trace.

Happy the weasel in the moonlit churchyard
    Twisting a vibrant thread
Of narrow life between the mounds that hide
    The important dead.

Close to the complex fabric of their world
    The small beasts live who shun
The spaces where the huge ones bellow, fight,
    And snore in the sun.

How admirable the modest and the frugal,
    The small, the neat, the furtive.
How troublesome the mammoths of the world,
    Gross and assertive.

Happy should we live in the interstices
    Of a declining age,
Even while the impudent masters of decision
    Trample and rage.

SOUTH COAST DWELLERS
IN WARTIME

Like footprints of angels on the floor of heaven
Starfish and cockle-shells encrust the shore.
Skimming fastidiously over your pink villas
Rapacious, with wings of snow, the gulls alight
On the red loam of the cliff-top behind the plough.
Over your airy world, airier still,
Moves the black shadow of the wings of death.
You raise your eyes from newspaper or from ironing.
Out at sea the foam-edge glints like teeth in a smile.
The ignorant crustaceans
In myriads pursue their minute desires.
Life improvises infinite variations
Upon this dual theme, the delicate and the cruel.

HONEYSUCKLE SMELL

What brings the sea-wind so far inland?
It is a memory of honeysuckle
Which nullifies the years between
This garden and those ragged hedges,
Teasing the nostrils, moistening the eyes,
Confronting me with you and you with me.

Child who crowned my head with flowers,
Could I have put the garland from your hands,
Could I have warned you
I was to be the godhead you projected,
I would have spared you this much pain
Nor seen you thus discomfited
Who used to be so confident and gay.

MISGIVINGS

Ask me no question now or any night,
Ask no question, dearest, and forgive,
If now and then I stop to hark
As the wind fidgets in the dark
Outside the window—if I have no ear
For you, but seem to hear

Something as an old fox gone to ground
Might hear a certain half-forgotten sound
Or stiffen at a scent which crept
About him as he slept.

Uneasiness like this can instantly
Turn all into a dream—
Yes, and make your eyes seem
Violets in woods irrevocably lost.

PAYSAGE

I know that silver trees beside the river
When first light thins a milk-and-water mist
Cannot be otherwise than calm and helpless
—A virgin grove.

Then why should such a picture disconcert me,
Flooding the mind with purposeless regret,
As if those leaves were Daphne's hair transformed?

GREENHALLOWS

All the omens were good, the air smelt of success.
The sun soared over the defeated mist.
I had broken no shoelace, shaved without mishap.
My toga swung handsomely.
The train bounded between the silver roofs.
A girl in muslin with a skipping-rope
Waved from a courtyard. The wires saluted me.
'Greenhallows'—pretty name. Reading between
The careful lines in the personal column
I visualised a sort of chauffeur-secretary
Reliable and relied on as I moved
Expertly among the week-end guests,
Good birth my passport, travel my education.
I thought of the starry-eyed, the exiles,
The handkerchiefs along the quay—
And now for me no more
The accordion in the sailors' café,
The olive-islands grey with anguish, blurred.
I smoothed my clothes
And straightened my new chaplet of acanthus.

Lawn-green are the halls in that superb mansion,
Sea-green the carpet sweeping up the stair
To where you hear in fancy
From nile-green bathrooms siren voices sing.
Somewhere amidst porcelain and laughter
You imagine the guests
Heavy-lipped, high-cheeked, beautiful,
Listening with their eyes.
To those on the sun-roof
Boys with indifferent classic brows carry soft drinks.

Out in the garden languid waters play,
In the house music from hidden strings.
Remote dynamos make power and light.
Birds of foreign plumage, coppery, dark,
Circle about the electric chandeliers.

I was left long alone, wondering
Whether it was really morning or evening,
Whether the servants had lied about the time.
How it was the murals were of my design
And why the signatures in the visitors' book—
Senators', athletes', film-stars' (even some
Of yours, my friends)—were all in my own writing!
As I entered, why had I felt distinctly
As if someone had just replaced
The ornaments by others of my choice?
Then what was it they had said in the village
About 'attempts' and 'interference'? Was that the
        reason
For the debris imperfectly concealed
Under a tarpaulin by the garage?
Why the fire in August? Why
The unmistakable odour of disinfectant?

A door clicks. Discreet feet
Ripple the sea-green floor.
'Mr Presumption? My name is Wheels.
Her ladyship will be down directly. In the meantime—
As I hand over my reference from the priest
I see it is marked with fingerprints of sweat.
My ears hum. A sound of sawing, then
An angel-voice, thin-souled like the wind
Threading a colonnade of icicles—
Mine! a record made at choir-school years ago

'I'm not quite well—I ought to catch the next train
    back.'
'Train? But there's no station—'
Lies! 'We had it moved
On account of the noise.' Falsehood! deceit!
The green walls swim apart, the floor rocks,
All revolves. Blackness . . . and then
A cool hand, something to drink, white and bitter.
My eyes open and see
The stone smile of a queen
The bust of Minerva on a public building
The Lady of Greenhallows.
My friends, pity me. You have been there
You have all been to Greenhallows in your time.
Yes, though you tore your diaries and re-tore them
And watched the fragments shrivel, you remember.
I need not tell you how I ran,
My chaplet fallen, my toga disarrayed.
I noticed the door was marked 'Out Patients'
And a man in a white coat raged and flapped.
The green vistas that deluded, you have seen them
And heard the mocking music that pursued me.
We shall keep, my friends, among us
This unshared secret, the shame and the elation.
One day shall we make, perhaps, together,
A journey without omens and mistrust the weather?

AEONS HENCE

When, aeons hence, they rediscover
The unregarded island I inhabit,
Will they not marvel
How life upon so bare a soil withstood
This testy climate and abrasive sea?

And when by excavation
My relics are exposed, my habits known,
How, perching on a ledge out of the wind,
I scraped a living, will they not admit
They've lost the secret of some things I did,
As making good pots from this gritty clay
And music from a certain kind of shells?

THE HAPPY BOY

It is the son of tears and want
Who learns to make the future grow,
The circle at the tunnel's end.
But the entirely happy child
Becomes a loiterer all his life,
Looking for the private glade
And the lost dell where he played.

29

MUSIC IN THE WOOD

Music there would be of horns far off.
Sombre and dolorous through the woods it came
To where we faltered in the darkening track.

The trees are taller now. Should I return,
That seminal music—would it still he heard,
Those notes again congeal my errant blood,
A cruel shiver at the spine recall
The wind lamenting in the perjured valley?
With what unclouded mind the man might then
Witness the marvel that perturbed the child.

INTROSPECTION

Curious how something quaint and long discarded
Revives a rapture you had thought forgotten.
Take in your hand this shell. The ear held close
Catches a whisper from the inward past.

It is a mouth singing secretly
Or a cave where restless water slides
Over the shingle; it is consciousness
Locked upon innocent experience.

You recall how downstairs seemed such a cave.
The after-bedtime music, the low voices
Were spells your mother and your father made;
The child listening at the stairhead, you.

Does not the circumstance amaze you now?
'Could it be I,' you say, 'who suffered such
Tumult on tumult of melody and feeling?
Was I so deeply moved? Could I be, still?'

It was your father rescued you so cold
So wide-eyed on the shore of sleep and wonder.
Bearing his strange child to bed he asked
What you ask now, could it be really you?

A hundred things could move you, many times
Drowned in that sea you came to life again.
Those vanished phases of experience
None knew, none knows but memory the creator.

These are the lips of memory. Lean close
Your ear and know what once you were.
Troubled by changed intensity,
Perplexed by what became of you,
Be certain that the imprisoned sea
Has other mysteries to speak of yet.

FOR YEARS WE TRACED

For years we traced the river back,
A month of swamps for two of scree.
The beasts all died, the boys turned back.
For years we had not said
'Above the next fall the promised view
The green, rewarding view.'
What we had seen no one said.

One struck the sun-cursed rock,
Recited fearing for his mind
Time and again the shepherd's dirge,
Less for the death he had in mind
Than for the Shakespeare phrase.

One kept, he says, before his eyes
A picture by a Spanish master,
A peasant's brooding eyes
And tilted lustrous wine.
I saw the columned temple in the haze
As its designer saw it first
Immaculate, finished in the sunset haze.

Bound in our spirit's isolation
These we felt we could appraise.
Bound by the thwarted enterprise
We thought we knew the worth of praise.
These, not the legendary land,
The impossible land towards the source,
Were what our vision played on,
And had been for years.

TWO MINDS

Stone-eyed, with a sculpture-lion look,
The old man in his garden stares
From centuries of correctitude.
His fine nostrils slightly note
The October bonfires of his neighbours;
His brow disdains
The charred fragments on his border.
I, hovering between the gravel and the turf,
Between talk and musing, glance
Now at my host and now at where
The tall flowers violet and blue
Grouped in perennial sisterhood
Surpass a seedsman's fantasy.

Seeing the many roofs of many neighbours
The half-made gardens of the more to come
And the old man aloof,
Sedate lineage scarce affronted,
I hover between two minds rejecting both:
The feeling of 'all this has been before,
It all happened to me long ago'—
Only a re-enacting
Could be so graphic, so composed—
The doubt that none the less
What is new is ineffectual
Since tenure of history
So long enjoyed not even death disputes.

THOUGHTS INDOORS

Never ask questions walking on a lawn.
The unanswered ones still bring the garden ghosts
 Too numerous already
To bandy them among the leaves till dawn.
 Let perfumes vain and sweet
 Wander there
 But in such presence-ridden air
Question no more for idlers to repeat.

Never ask questions off the shore of sleep.
The nodding masts would bear you into port.
 Voyaging-time is over.
Let speculations till the morning keep.
 Away from this smooth shore
 Are doubtful seas.
 Think if you will of certainties,
But better now to sleep and think no more.

Ask questions at your hearth, the place of answers.
Think where thoughts end in thought, not ghosts or
 sleep,
 Where you alone are hearer
And round your books the moths are heedless dancers.
 Then moths at last expel
 To ghosts and flowers
 And give to sleep the sleepy hours
When your four walls have nothing more to tell.

THE PICTURE IN THE MIST

Peace now, not futility,
I call the picture in the mist,
The vacant, gentle landscape which
I had and had not seen before.

Although my usual vision marks
The mire and dung upon the track
I see not prints of slithering hooves
But the firm foothold underneath.

The haystack by the standing pools
Which loneliness had misconceived
As desolate and miserable
Has now become a place of shelter.

It is because you, silent there
While the rain trickled down your face
Searched me with your improvident smile
Conscious of no cause nor end.

It is because your being there
And your so very present look
Affirmed for me the immediate scene,
Made memory of the fatal one,

That a surrounding picture-sense
Can to my mind a message bring
Of peace and standing on firm ground
Instead of emptiness half-seen.

VISITORS TO THE WATERFALL

They see the rowan trees above the fall,
    The broken rainbow at its base.
Moistened by spray they scale the mountain wall;
        Their footsteps do not stumble,
        Because almost a grace
        Is given by such elation
As violence with grandeur causes them,
    When stunned past exclamation
They hear the foam hiss and the waters tumble.

They will be safely down before the dark
    And home before the summer ends.
The scarlet berries and the coloured arc,
        The cataclysm and thunder
        They will describe to friends
        And photographs renew.
Then which of them would be surprised to feel
    His cheek grow cold with dew,
His pulse quicken, his breath stop short for wonder?

They will not see the fragile rainbow fade
    The instant that the sun goes down.
Not dark nor autumn will their scene invade;
        They will not see the red
        Transform to shrivelled brown,
        The rowan-berries fall
Of no account into unfertile crannies.
    But they will picture all
As it is, momentary, and nothing dead.

After the summer drought they will not hear
   The streams fail and the roar subside.
Then through the dwindling waters hard and clear
     The naked rock will show
     Which now the waters hide.
     Such the true nature is
Of this bright mountain country—at its heart
     A sunless gorge. But this
For their vision's sake must visitors not know.

A MATTER OF DISCIPLINE

Paunch foremost, shambling, dilatory,
The school porter came to the school play.
Although we call him sergeant-major
Nothing of him now is military
Except perhaps his waxed moustaches.
But when he saw those mimic soldiers,
The slovenly parade-ground antics,
And heard the callow actors mock
The old commands, who knows what stirred
Of an obscure allegiance hidden
In his slack nerves, to protest bidden?
Perhaps an instant's brief suspension
Of many years' passivity
His unused muscles mobilised
To stand correctly to attention.

The Password
1952

THE PASSWORD

If you have seen the error of the moth,
    The white moth stumbling through the starless
        night,
And heard, though dumb, the entreaty of her wings
    Bruised and defeated in your treadmill light;

If you have seen how lamplight from a room
    Falls on the coloured flowers and the grass,
Warm as a promise, private as a smile,
    Touching as sorrow in a looking-glass;

If, on a summer night, from distant strings
    Wordless nostalgia of a serenade
Hints in your ear a refuge out of time
    Where the innocent need not be afraid—

O if the moth, the lamplight and the music,
    If these are tokens between me and you,
There needs no password to our understanding
    And no formality to let you through.

THE TREE OF LIFE

I shared my garden with the tree of life,
  In whose bewildering and populous maze
Delicious birds conspired incessantly
  To steal and squander all my earnest days.

And in my room at night and in my ears
  The cunning voices of the leaves would creep.
Riddling predictions, twilight menaces
  Twitched the uneasy curtains of my sleep.

I strove one night beneath a murderer's moon
  With sharpest stroke and self-destructive rage
To fell the monster or at least some boughs
  For it was proud and obdurate with age.

And when it groaned at my demented blows
  And shuddered fearfully from bole to bud,
I saw with cry of horror on my breath
  The ground below was overrun with blood.

I share my garden with the deathless tree.
  My days and nights those voices still entrap.
What was the image by the storm-tossed moon?
  The tree of life has blood instead of sap.

THE NEWCOMER

They who minister to the cattle of this land
   And side by side the deliberate furrows laid
Lounge now at ease beneath the merciful blue
   In the kneeling elm trees' or the hedgerow's shade.
My steps beside the fields of County Down
   They marked with curious but encouraging eye,
And the close hedges between which I walked
   Seemed to me equally kind and equally shy.

Softly I went, as if to overhear
   A hidden life beneath the moss and fern,
But caught only the random tunes of birds
   Whose names, regretfully, I could never learn.
Only the rooks cantankerous overhead
   And roosters unambiguously professed
A pastoral order long established there
   In which I moved half inmate and half guest.

And when the unobtrusive scent of briar,
   Honeysuckle, elderberry and drying hay
From grove and pasture in unseen procession
   Came out to greet the traveller on his way,
It was as if the gentlest of the dead
   Welcomed the latest comer to their land,
Spectre to spectre nodding reassurance
   And proffering their gifts with timid hand.

VOICES LOUD AND LOW

The rainstorm stretched its harp across the sky;
The Druid played beneath the weeping cloud.
I heard his music roll among the hills
In modulation passionate and loud.

I heard the lake for ever unappeased,
The singing swan when daylight rose and fled;
I heard the chattering of the chestnut bough,
And the moon's consolation to the dead.

Painful it is to keep such secrets secret,
And yet to whom and how communicate?
Fool, knave and harlot recognise the prophet
Only with head presented on a plate.

HAD I PASSION TO MATCH MY SKILL

Had I passion to match my skill,
I would not hear the worm complain,
The worm that frets and mumbles still
In the corridors of my brain.

The flames that burn inside my heart,
On what fuel do they feed?
I the mystery would impart,
Had I skill to match my need.

Had I passion and skill
To match my daring will,
I would rise and seek
The stony path that scales the virgin peak.

Between my hands I hold my brain,
Between my ribs I nurse a fire;
Beyond my utmost step remain
The summits where the goats aspire.

Inside my brain the worm revolves,
The heart consumes inside my breast;
And so I sit, and nothing solves
The puzzles that are not expressed.

LET NONE LAMENT ACTAEON

Why should my lips, when I recall your lips,
   Shape the cry 'Artemis, O Artemis'?
Why should your lips suggest a wound, a bow,
   A crescent knife unsheathed—and not a kiss?

Why should your voice, that is so bright a singer,
   Now in my recollection seem to flow
Not from a source in some reviving pasture
   But from a mortal wilderness of snow?

And on that snow the hoofprints and the blood
   Point where the torn stag limped away to die;
The hunter's ghost still feels the foetid breath
   And hears the avenging dogs' horrific cry.

Let none lament Actaeon. Better to say:
   'Stabbed by the smile of Artemis, there died
One who was happy in his own defeat,
   Leaving her hounds the gobbets of his pride.'

THE SWAN

Against the unrelenting stream,
   Ignoring sunset's angry hour,
Floated the miraculous swan,
   And in her beak a single flower.

My eyes reflected sunset's flush;
   Resentful on the bank I cried:
'Dishonoured queen of spite and greed,
   Take hence your emblem with your pride.'

But she sailed on in constancy
   And stopped beside me on the flood.
I saw the flower, a thornless rose,
   Was dark and crimson as her blood.

And looking on her there I guessed
   That she was miracle indeed,
A swan for grace and royalty
   Yet knowing neither scorn nor greed.

She bent her head upon the bank
   And laying all her pride apart
She gave her rose into my hand.
   My falling tears found out its heart.

THE END OF THE STORY

Whether they told him tales or he contrived them,
　It was all one: his head was big with myth,
Big, that is, for a boy's; he was the king,
　The hero, and the friend they counselled with.

He was the prince who, straying from his fellows,
　Pursued the wounded hare into the brake,
And saw a shadowy girl a-huddle there,
　Her thin face streaked with tears for its sake.

He would have been the creature if he could,
　Bloody against her breast; his heart was quick;
Her eyes were unforgettable with pity;
　The hare's, like peeled blue grapes, were dull and
　　thick.

He was the prisoner in the heartless tower,
　Dry-eyed from grief, like an exhausted sea;
And through his granite-pillowed nightmare walked
　The gaoler's daughter with the purloined key.

He was the hungry exile by the river,
　Haunting the cities of a foreign land,
To whom the apple-seller on the bridge
　Tendered the fruits of her restoring hand.

He was a spectre in a timeless desert
　Choking and harsh like ashes on the breath.

And when he died, the queen of that sad realm
    Stretched out her hand and said, 'It is not death.

'It is not death, but love,' and raised him up.
    Not as a stranger then he stood before her.
He knew her eyes, and felt her touch, and kissed her;
    And on that day consented to adore her.

Hers were the eyes that he had seen in boyhood,
    Desolate under the hawthorn long ago;
Her lips had called to him in prison softly;
    Her hand had fed him on the bridge of woe.

'What then is death?' he asked, as one who saw
    Petal and apple from the same bough shaken.
Lost in each other's presence, neither knew
    If love was something given or something taken.

THE ROSE AND STAR

If you would sing your songs at the Rose and Star,
   You will find company there of a sort, and wine;
Though the star is tarnished and the rose outmoded,
   It is an ancient and honourable sign.

If you would sing there, provide yourself with tunes
   For which you must barter with the Queen of Hell,
She will demand the apples from your pack,
   Gold out of your pocket, your straight sword as well.

If you would gain a hearing, you must have them,
   Even though it take the heart out of your breast;
Blind and blind-drunk was the old Irish fiddler
   From whom the devil her husband stole the best.

That company of loungers, thieves and girls
   Will not substantially repay devotion;
But think your song rewarded if you note
   A hush, a sigh, a shuffle of emotion.

One there I knew who, desperate and young,
   Sold the black Queen his breath, and won the prize;
It was a gold crown worked by his false mistress
   From her own smiles, with diamonds from her eyes.

If you would sing your songs at the Rose and Star,
   You would find company there of a sort, and wine;
Though birds have fouled the star and the rose is
     worm-holed,
   It is an ancient and honourable sign.

LEAVING TOWN

It was impossible to leave the town.
Bumping across a maze of obsolete rails
Three times we reached the gasworks and reversed.
We could not get away from the canal;
Dead cats, dead hopes, in those grey deeps immersed,
Over our efforts breathed a spectral prayer.
The cattle-market and the gospel-hall
Returned like fictions of our own despair,
And like Hesperides the suburbs seemed,
Shining far off towards the guiltless fields.
We finished in a little cul-de-sac
Where on the pavement sat a ragged girl
Mourning beside a jug-and-bottle entrance.
Once more we turned the car and started back.

IN THE TRAIN

She is the passenger with restless eyes
Who twists the ticket in her black-gloved fingers.
None knows what calculation, what surmise
Disturb her as the train jerks on or lingers.
Above the eyes her brow is smooth and yellow.
'I grant,' her silence says, 'that all I planned
Has been like something graven in the sand,
But tell me how *your* schemes work out, my fellow.'

IN THE CLUBHOUSE

In the clubhouse are exchanged banalities,
    Also commercial privileges. A lavish odour
Circles the heads of houses when they scheme;
    And the river of time flows down like brandy-and-
        soda.

The cleverest heads will be crowned with genuine
        gold,
    Crowns of gold for the strongest. No one supposes
That she behind the bar is a queen incognita
    And will reward the loser with a crown of wild
        roses.

Not on a white liner she came, first class,
    From Jamaica, Manila, Kenya or the west—
No, but from blue Sicilian fields with her head full
    Of doves in the silver trees telling of rest.

THE PRISONERS

Somehow we never escaped
    Into the sunlight,
Though the gates were always unbarred
    And the warders tight.
For the sketches on the walls
    Were to our liking,
And squeaks from the torture-cell
    Most satisfying.

WATERS OF LIFE

The hasting dark has driven home
Father and daughter, mother, child,
Who by this fecund spring since noon
Have chattered, scolded, wept and smiled.

The feet that loitered by the stream
And voices on the wind have fled.
The leaves that screen the dormant birds
To no one mutter overhead:

'The waters of the stream of life
Are tears that flow from women's eyes.
He thirsts again that drinks this spring,
But if he will not drink he dies.'

SONG

[*Music, they said*]

Music, they said, built cities
That wore their bells like flowers;
Flowers, I thought, could heal
The hurt of savage hours.
But this was all a fiction:
It was the fact of you
That woke me from the music
Whence flowers and cities grew.

A FIRE I LIT

A fire I lit to warm my hands
   Blazed out and leapt upon the floor.
It burnt to ashes my tall house
   And left me colder than before.

THE LITTLE BROTHER

God! how they plagued his life, the three damned
    sisters,
Throwing stones at him out of the cherry trees,
Pulling his hair, smudging his exercises,
Whispering. How passionately he sees
His spilt minnows flounder in the grass.

There will be sisters subtler far than these,
Baleful and dark, with slender, cared-for hands,
Who will not smirk and babble in the trees,
But feed him with sweet words and provocations,
And in his sleep practise their sorceries,
Appearing in the form of ragged clouds
And at the corners of malignant seas.

As with his wounded life he goes alone
To the world's end, where even tears freeze,
He will in bitter memory and remorse
Hear the lost sisters innocently tease.

OLD CRABBED MEN

This old crabbed man, with his wrinkled, fusty
    clothes
And his offensive smell—who would suppose
That in his day he invented a new rose
Exciting still the fastidious eye and nose?

That old crabbed man, sloven of speech and dress,
Was once known among women—who would now
    guess?—
As a lover of the most perfect address,
Reducing the stubbornest beauty to nakedness.

This old crabbed man, pattering and absurd,
With a falsetto voice—which of you has heard
How in his youth he mastered the lyric word?
His unflawed verse spoke like a March bird.

BEATA

Since histories of darkness and of blood
　Are all they ask, so I may tell them how
You led me groping through the cruel wood
　And thorny branches snapped against my brow.

Disgusting fancies of my solitude
　On ragged wing, dreadful at close of day,
Voracious phantoms that had long pursued—
　May I not tell how these you charmed away?

Then through the memory of that dream you spoke:
　But by what ministrations and what spell
You brought me back to life when I awoke
　Language of blood and darkness does not tell.

YOU IN ANGER

You in your anger tried to make us new,
　To cancel all the warmth and loving-kindness
With which maturing time has joined us two,
　And re-infect love with its former blindness.

It was as if you said, 'I am a stranger;
　Unknown we face each other, woman and man.
We stand, as once we stood, in mortal danger;
　Risk everything, as I do, if you can.'

Then do not now repent your wilful scorn;
  Although in that black hour I hated you,
Yet in that hour, love, was my love re-born;
  When you in anger tried to make us new.

THE SPINNER

The spinner with her smile involves
The sinews of the stander-by,
And with her pliant hands she twines
His vital organs in her thread.
Her foot beats out his dance of death,
The wheel revolves and is his fate.
Her eyes regard the dwindling fleece;
His mind is netted in her hair,
And questions 'Is it love or hate?'
As half she sings and half she smiles,
And looks as if he were not there.
The wheel revolves and is his fate.

FRAGMENTS OF A LANDSCAPE

The uninhabitable moon
Rejects her lifelong worshippers
Who long since knelt upon the shore
Raising their arms for pity and relief
Until they flaked to skeletons.

We walked together on the strand
Eye in eye and hand in hand.
You could not see my mouth was full of sand,
Like a blind statue that could no more stand.
You could not hear the waves that beat
Tumultuous in the chambers of my heart,
Forcing their walls apart,
Till I had no desire except to be
One with the kneeling bones
Among the seabirds and the seaworn stones.

THEIR SPECTRES RISE

Their spectres rise in mockery from the place
Where I passed by them twenty years ago,
Their long legs dancing softly to and fro.
Why did the proud scholar cast down his face?
How for a book could he neglect them so?
Their spectres rise in mockery from the place

Where I passed by them twenty years ago.
Often I see them in their former grace.
Surely, they say, such a scholar should know
Backwards he cannot make the river flow.
Their spectres rise in mockery from the place
Where I passed by them twenty years ago,
Their long legs dancing softly to and fro.

THIS IS YOUR ELEGY

This is your elegy, the grey sea grieving—
This and the gulls' disconsolate reply.
Beyond your hearing is their derelict cry.

Now every wave reminds me of your leaving.
There is no houseless bird more lost than I.
This is your elegy, the grey sea grieving—
This and the gulls' disconsolate reply.

To end your absence and your unbelieving
With yet one more 'I love you', I would try
To call my sea-bird back from the cold sky.
This is your elegy, the grey sea grieving—
This and the gulls' disconsolate reply.
Beyond your hearing is their derelict cry.

NOVELS I HAVE NEVER WRITTEN

From novels I have never written
The ghosts have long departed,
Leaving tenantless the Sussex country houses
And the palazzo steps brown with moss.
Only the foundations remain
On which were to have risen
The towers and cloisters of the fatal school.
In the unfinished rooms
The conversations have shivered into silence.
The moving incidents,
The revealing situations,
The moments of profound psychological insight—
All are lost, unwanted,
Like garden furniture rusting in a summer-house.
All the ghosts have departed, unaccounted for,
Some perhaps for South America,
Others to get what employment they can
As car-park attendants and waiters in seaside hotels,
Or they have simply died.

Only the disconsolate hero survives,
Sitting on an upturned packing-case in an empty
     house,
With the electricity and the telephone cut off,
Nothing to eat, no money, and nowhere to go.
Too round a character to disappear quietly,
Too big a man to be pensioned off or eased into a
     sinecure.
Presently, perhaps, he will reappear in Oxford
As one of those dusty, forgotten dons whom I have
     heard

Talking to themselves in the High,
Or a faded roué living on the Côte d'Azur
On the savings of a discarded opera-singer—
Someone who can sustain the pretence
Of having been influential in former days,
The intimate of writers, friend of diplomats . . .

THE STONE GENTLEMAN

Let us move the stone gentleman to the toadstool
    wood:
Too long has he disapproved in our market-place.
Within the manifold stone creases of his frock-coat
    Let the woodlouse harbour and thrive.

Let the hamadryads wreath him with bryony,
The scrolled fern-fronds greenly fantasticate,
And sappy etiolations cluster damply
    About the paternal knee.

Them the abrupt, blank eyes will not offend.
The civic brow and raised, suppressive hand
Unchallenged and without affront shall manage
    The republic of tall spiders.

PRIMADONNA

Age cannot wither her, for youth has done it;
But the vicissitudes of mortal progress
May yet transform a bitch into an ogress.

Observe without dismay the handsome face.
The yellow teeth and yellow conjunctiva,
The mouth agleam with lipstick and saliva

And marked with vices she has only dreamed,
Reveal a certain paralysing charm
Like that of the stone heads on Notre Dame.

On those above, and far enough below,
She turns a wet, ingratiating smile,
A voice to wheedle, flatter and beguile.

But read between the lines, the face is harsh;
The smile is but the mirror of a mind
By flagellation-fantasies refined.

Let but some near-subordinate rebel—
How quickly vanishes the obsequious leer
And the cajoling voice becomes a sneer.

It is her pride to call a spade a spade,
And when her spade bisects the offending worm,
It is her joy to see the pieces squirm.

Better be in the wrong than prove her wrong.
Then hear her bluster, bully, rage and fret,
And stamp and strut and play the martinet.

But let bad luck assail her, or self-doubt,
Then see the ego droop, the spirit sink,
Until restored by flattery or drink.

COUNSEL TO BOYS

At Holy Trinity beside the quay
   The grey one touched my arm and pointed up.
'Some poor soul going home,' she said to me.

And in her eyes I saw the mourners pass
   And with her parchment ears I heard the chant
Raised for the dead bound in with lacquered brass.

A sea-wind like the passage of a soul
   Fluttered her torn remains and she was gone.
To all alike comes at the end such dole.

Therefore, rash youngster on the bridge at play
   Near where the old men lean and fish for nothing,
Better than do as they do, I would say,

Since all are paid their funerary verses,
   Better it is to study to grow rich
And own at last a fleet of plated hearses.

How better serve the poor ones of your city
   Than carry them in decent splendour home,
And thus on all grey ragged souls take pity?

'A LETTER TO POSTERITY'

(SUGGESTED BY A RADIO SERIES UNDER THAT TITLE)

This I would say. I see you perfectly
In your unfashionable favourite chair,
With knees drawn up and cheek on fist, your page
Shadowed by indeterminate brown hair.

You read of us perhaps, or think of him,
The unmitigable man who steals your mind;
I hear you sigh, and see you smile, and wonder
What comedy in us or him you find.

We have philosophers, and so have you.
'Our age' they say, not knowing what they mean;
But I can tell you, dear, what our age is,
What yours is too, and others all have been.

Cities and ships we purpose for your ease,
To see you grateful, smiling in your chair;
If we forget, or fail, or you turn peevish,
We break and burn in fury of despair.

Ask that dark man who blunders through your
        thoughts
Why from the precipice he brings you flowers;
Smile on him if you can: only your smile
Can make his age a better age than ours.

GOOD-BYE AT CARTHAGE

Good-bye is spoken on the quay;
The white wake bears away my dear.
The anguish of this desert sea
Will never trouble that proud ear;
And my salt sorrow is to me
As is the ocean to the tear.

CATULLUS TO LESBIA

I tell you, Lesbia, life is love,
Though rumbling dotards disapprove
    And chew their beards in spite.
For ever shines the blessed sun,
But we have little space to run,
And after our brief day is done,
    How long will be the night.

So kiss me, kiss me, kiss me, sweet.
Kiss me neither once nor twice,
But kiss me several hundred times
    And then the tale repeat.
A thousand, then a thousand times,
    And that will not suffice—
A thousand, then a hundred more,
And after many thousand kisses
    We'll forget the score,

In case some mad misanthropist,
Hearing how many times we've kissed,
Should bring down curses on our heads
   To think what he has missed.

THE RETROVERT

'I never hear'—so Charles Lamb tells—
'The joyful sound of New Year bells
Without a look towards the past.'

Perhaps each year he heard again
His mother's scream, and saw the knife
That kept him prisoner all his life
In his poor sister's haunted brain.

POET OF BIRDS

J C R

Lost bird, dead bird, dove, peacock, nightingale—
They fly and cry their way through all your page.
If it is liberty they symbolise,
How were you prisoner then, and in what cage?

The Talking Skull
1958

TO NORMAN CAMERON 1905–1953

I asked the river-god a song
With which to mourn your fallen head.
No answer: but a low wind crept
About the stones of his dry bed.

The fingers of insomnia
Turning the pages of self-hate
Are like the incurious wind that stirred
The papery reeds on that estate.

In other days I knew the god
Who flashed and chuckled in the sun.
Where has he taken now his moods
Of shadow and his sense of fun?

The requiem I might have had
From him you would have understood:
Just as you also understood
How hard a thing it is, though good,

To hold your tongue and wait your time
When there is nothing to be said.
I know it now: I knew you both
But he is gone, and you are dead.

Even the wind has died; no sound
In this dull air is born to live;
So I my desperate silences
To you my friend and poet give.

THE SAVAGE MOON

A Meditation on John Clare

I

I saw a dead tree, and the moon beyond,
Low in the sky, untroubled, full and round;
Nearer, a thin rain's diorama fell
And blurred the surface of the brimming pond.

I searched the moon, the water, and the tree.
They had no meaning, and my heart was full.
The smug Gioconda moon hoarded her secrets.
It was as if one whom I could not see

Passed and re-passed, desiring speech with me.
I would have been glad even to feel afraid.
His urgency oppressed me, catching only
Meaningless gestures of the withered tree.

Neither the wind nor rain spoke then; and I,
Marking this moonward gesture of dead limbs,
Felt only the sense of unexplained disquiet
And let the stranger-spirit pass me by.

And in that inauspicious Midland shire
Where he was born, and where his spirit haunts,
Lank girls in raincoats and unthinking youths,
Searching the same moon with the same desire,
Were troubled then by his uneasy passage,
As if they felt a touch upon the sleeve,
As if they heard a voice upon the air
That sighed to be delivered of its message.

72

II

The shadow of that small man haunts me still.
I see him unappeased,
His russet form stumping the road uphill,
Weathered, yet pale of face, his forehead's height
Unusual, his blue eyes dangerously bright.

Continually he haunts me, unappeased
Among the beanfields and the cottage rows.
Rhyming and scribbling without cease he goes,
Catching words from the wind,
From the air fanning his high cheek
Where the fever glows.
A meadow brook flows in his mind like rhythm.
He lifts his head to the autumn sky
For a colour or a look.
A rhyme chimes in his ear like Glinton bells;
His nostrils catch a scent from the lea
Where sweet briar smells.
Perhaps you have seen
The toss of a flower's head in the breeze,
The tones of a stone wall,
The motion of hens running for corn,
Of bird's wings settling to roost,
A farm dog's tail as his master's steps are heard;
You have seen
Bees entering flower-heads,
Cattle awaiting a storm,
Willow leaves greying in the wind—
All these he has noted and discovered.

What moves him as he moves among the fields?

Everything he has seen,
Not this or that phenomenon of nature
But all the minutiae of flower and insect,
Infant bird, bird's nest, and bird's egg;
Every sound he has heard,
Every sound that comes on the wind
From water, tree, or beast.
What moves him as he moves among these things?
What haunts him, haunting these precious scenes?
Why
Does a lark's wing lift him to the sky,
A dragon-fly
Lead him along the glittering shallows?
What gave him the passion
To put in writing heat, cold,
Frost, snow, drought, rain,
All the effects of climate and of season?
What moved him as he moved about the fields?

III

It was no mild Gioconda moon that shone
Over his father's roof when he was born.
It was a bloody and a terrible one
Crying destruction on the poor man's son.

Over him there was bloody warfare done—
Warfare all night between the wrathful moon
And the green world of men. Such was her power
That in this strife of planets the moon won.

The world would have had him labour, slave to the
    sun,
To dig, and sow, and harvest, year by year,

74

If not content, then stoical; not known
Beyond the parish bounds. But the moon won.

That moon in many guises ruled him. Fame
Tempted him like a sin; even applause
Fell in a shower of guineas on his head,
And titled Byron might have been his name.

That moon in many guises ruled him. Green
And smiling nature led his feet astray.
He was the vagrant watcher in the shade,
The ruminant amidst the woodland scene.

That moon in many guises ruled him. Verse
Beguiled him morning and evening, boy and man;
No help, the world would vanish when he knew
The rhyming fit was on him like a curse,

That moon in many guises ruled him. Love,
Virgin and unrewarded, went before him;
And by the name of Mary Joyce possessed
The earth below, the feathered air above.

His stormy moon approved the fourfold cheat.
The voice of water promising no thirst,
And ancient bird-song that remembered Eden
This was the flattering music of deceit.

Fame was the evil angel and the good,
Guiding him on and then abandoning.
He might in fancy be the rhyming lord
While his doomed wife and children cried for food.

Love touched his growing senses at the root,
Making him quick to note the shape of leaves,
The sound of insects' wings, the smell of grass,
The timid snail upon the hawthorn shoot.

Rejected love became self-love, and then
Self-pity; his heart was every hunted creature's;
He was the limping hare, he was the badger
Harried to death at last by dogs and men.

Poetry, sternest guardian, constant friend,
Subtlest betrayer, charmed his boyhood hours,
Cost him the world, no less; but visited
The insane prison of his homeless end.

Was it ambition or the savage moon
Which made this vampire poetry his mistress,
To charm his hearing with the hum of bees
And craze him with the night wind's frantic tune?

IV

Man is born homeless, and the search for home
Creates him and destroys him, hour by hour.
Some, like poor Keats, by the gambling furies
Are marked for quick death; some for life-in-death.
Of these was Clare:
Half a life of life-in-death
The gambling furies dealt for him.
Half a life
Of near oblivion and obscurity,
Of captive non-identity,
Divided him from home.

The place of darkness whispered 'Come',
The answer from his breast must wait.
The land of shadows hour by hour
Half a lifetime he must tread.
For certain objects of their own
His guardian demons led him through
The weary maze of madness and despair.
Assured of nothing—neither God,
Nor his own self, nor mortal love,—
For half a life he moved alone
About a world of fantasy and myth,
Moon-lit, shaken by nightmare winds,
And by the comfortless spectres of unreason.

He who had dreamed beyond most common dreams,
Had taken great ones' favour for true praise
Had had a noble patron, heard curious ladies' coaches
Grate on the road outside his cottage door—
How could he ever make his home again
Under a labourer's roof, his wife a drudge,
His ragged children always sick or dying?
Yet to this home I see him trudge alone
Four days upon a pennyworth of bread,
A runaway from a private mental home,
His feet bleeding, his spirit drained of hope.
Already in her grave, unknown to him,
It was his virgin bride that drew him on.
Home no more home to him, nowhere was left
But the black friendless prison of his thought,
And no one to go bail for him but death.

V

I am left with a recollection of the moon
Sailing the ragged spaces between trees
Amid whose branches the birds build and tune.

I have seen trees cut down that have stood long
    weathers
And in some fork a bird's abandoned nest,
A coil of dried grass round a core of feathers.

And I have thought: Where flew the bird and its
    young?
That mating and building—to what end did it come?
On what wind, soundless now, trembles that song?

The cottage fireside and the dead girl's breast,
The enclosed pastures, the trees' creative shade—
These were the lunatic poet's ruined nest.

Yet from his passion flowed the happy verse,
And the huge winds are busy with it still.
I ask the savage moon, was ever worse

Thrown by brute fate on undefended head?
You who have searched the pathless polar sky,
Whose blue fire burns the cities of the dead,

Streaming through broken traceries of stone,
You who have heard, indifferent as time,
All bitter cries wrung from the very bone—
Is poetry a punishment or a crime?

THE FIELD OF LIES

But it was death he looked for in the field of lies,
Naming it love.
His thoughts reached down
Below the roots of the convolvulus.

Now, I suppose, the nettles breed and wave
Over his cenotaph, the bank they lay on.
A child that blows a dandelion-head
Knows more of time
Than any lovers murmuring 'For ever'.

Every seed entombs a shattered flower,
In every word a lie:
There is the truth of it.
The dew is cold,
And the moon quits the sky she does not love.
There is no metaphor for her indifference.

MIRANDA

Our revels now are ended. While you can,
　Enjoy her, Ferdinand. She will be true,
So long as you remain the only man.
　In Naples she will learn a thing or two.

ONCE AND NOW

Once, crossing by giant stones the brown water,
I remembered the king and his banished daughter.
A sad wind crept out of the hazel wood,
And in my eyes the unreasonable tears stood.

Once, in a sonata a broken phrase
Made me aware of dancers in a maze,
Of flutes and lanterns in the hall under the hill;
Again my eyes were wet and the air chill.

There is no ghost-dance now, no sleeping prince;
The tattered girl I have not remembered since.
Through music's labyrinth no strange airs speak;
No tears over the brown stream moisten my cheek.

LYRIC

Voices on the feathered air
Prey upon the lover's ear.
'Criticise her face or mind,
Praise the fashion of her hair.
Do not ask her to be kind,
Do not let her know you care.
Idle with her half a day;
Do not let her see despair
Eat your doting heart away.
Do not ask her to be kind

Or expect her to be true.
Freely she will give each gift.
If she play at cards with you,
Remember that she wants to lose
By her own dishonest shift,
Not by your victorious ruse.'
Heedless on the lover's ear,
Voices from the feathered air,
Empty voices call 'Beware!'

THIS MOOD OF MURDER

Say who brought murder to the quiet street,
To read his guilt in their white eyes
And in the acceleration of their feet:
Say who brought murder to the quiet street
And I will say my name.
     You should look pale
To hear the bells' resentful beat
Tolling, tolling his retreat.
You should look pale to understand his tale
In their white eyes and ticking feet.
Say who brought murder to the quiet street
And I will say my name.
     But should you pale
To meet his accomplice in your looking-glass,
Then go to bed alone with one who spread
This mood of murder in a quiet street.

THREE POEMS AFTER CATULLUS

I

Num te leœna

What lioness that roamed the Libyan waste
   Or raucous Scylla barking from her womb
Bore you, she-monster of the stony will?
   For when in the extremity of doom
Your vassal calls, you hold his words in scorn.
Too savage heart, of what beast were you born?

II

Odi et amo

I hate: yet where I hate, I love.
   You ask me why: I cannot tell.
But this I know—I feel it so,
   And suffer all the pangs of hell.

III

Lesbia illa

Think of it, Caelius, only think, my friend:
   Lesbia, that Lesbia, Lesbia our dearest,
   She whom Catullus better than his nearest
Better than his own soul loved without end,
Now where the noblest sons of Rome explore
Rome's dirtiest backstreets, there she plays the
    whore.

'AND SO THEY CAME TO LIVE AT DAFFODIL WATER'

'And so they came to live at Daffodil Water.'
Such were the words that fell as by dictation
Into the cloud of my preoccupation,
And one by one they fluttered down like leaves,
Touching me with their strange illumination—
Like leaves the girls would catch at Butler's Cross
To bring themselves good luck, each leaf a year.

'And so they came to live at Daffodil Water.'
A grey-green light of depths that do not stir
Beneath the unfledged ash-bough's contemplation
Touches me now as I transcribe the words.
Such were the depths perhaps where Hylas drowned,
Such were the wreaths his temptresses would wear.
But who are *they* who came to shelter there
And live obscurely by that leaf-light crowned,
Patiently mending their storm-shattered minds?

Who came to live in grace at Daffodil Water,
And why they sheltered there and from what storm,
Neither the voice that speaks through my abstraction
Nor my own fantasy serves to inform.

OLD AND YOUNG

Let the old inherit moonlight and sweet hay.
  Crazed with their fantasies of unachievement,
They falter in the way,
  And all is doubt and darkness and bereavement.

The young ask no such atmospheric grace.
  They know the certainties of lip and finger.
Each other's time and space,
  By no blanched hedgerows do they need to linger.

But the old walk alone and in despair;
  So let the moonlight unperplex their view,
And let the perfumed air
  Remind them of the world they think they knew.

FAMILY FACES

Between his snapshot children's faces
And snapshot faces of their father's childhood
The starer in the glass sees one disowned
By both old pictures and new children.
'Yes, I am you,' the face says back at him.
'Living its snapshot moments, that dead face
Disowns you. It has no heir but these—
These are the snapshot children of no father.
You and I with neither heirs nor forebears—
Domiciled together until we die
Let us know one another, you and I.'

BOTTOM'S DREAM

His hands move absently across the threads
   Beneath the foolish radiance of his face.
The rational Athenians look askance
   At the old weaver in the market-place.

How could he make them credit what he saw,
   Or dreamed, by moonshine in the woodland green,
When in his youthful, mad, midsummer time
   He lay all night beside the fairy queen?

ON A POET

E.B. 1896–1973

Having no Celtic bombast in his blood,
Nor dipsomaniac rage, nor very much
To give his time of what his time expected,
He saw his Muse, slight thing, by most neglected.

She was no exhibitionist, and he,
With only the Queen of Elfland's gift to Thomas,
Could not afford to school her in the taste
For stolen gauds and ornaments of paste.

When he is dead and his best phrases stored
With Clare's and Hardy's in the book of gold,
She with her unpresuming Saxon grace
In the Queen's retinue will take her place.

THE TALK

They talked of Dr Graham and the Church,
And William Moss the Labour candidate.
I thought how once I would have thought of you,
Of Dido's tears and of the shears of fate.

I would have thought of you and how you spoke
Of Picquette in her dress of cobweb-grey,
And of the six fauns' eyes between the saplings—
The lost girls, and the bad man in the play.

But when I thought of what I should recall,
Feeling, regret, and memory I had none.
Treason is absolute; it need not be
Treason to anything or anyone.

So with a sense of treason overhead
Clouding my mind, I followed the debate.
We talked of Dr Graham and the Church.
We talked of Moss the Labour candidate.

PERSEPHONE IN HADES

Though sculptures in a gallery
Clay forms and marble attitudes
Oppress the gazer with a sense of death,
Amid such things who has not some time seen
A broken figure or a figurine
Move suddenly from the stillness like a dancer
Or an emboldened bird finding the sun?

Stone houses in a town of streets
Are habitations of the dead.
Stone towers uphold a suffocating sky.
Yet walking in such streets, from such a tower
I have heard bell-notes dropping like a shower
Into the parched air, a shower of bells
Dropping like silver in a blind man's hand.

Statues and ghosts are resident
In Hades' songless galleries
Where I too haunt, a shade among the shades.
But like a dancer or a bird she came,
Princess of life, Persephone her name,
And like a sudden peal of bells she seemed
Whose tongues were unlocked prisoners crazed with
      joy.

BABYLONIAN FRAGMENT

Pyramus and Thisbe

The moon is tangled in the mulberry boughs
Where the white pigeon cried itself to sleep.
These lovers neighbouring in Babylon
Feared the waste places past their walls of clay.
The lion roamed the world outside their kiss—
The kiss that cracked the wall between their hearts.
Because they would not be immured in clay
These met destruction by the lion's shadow.
So now the mulberry tree is stained with blood
And the white bird is inconsolable.

AN ACADEMIC

How sad, they think, to see him homing nightly
In converse with himself across the quad,
Down by the river and the railway arch
To his gaunt villa and his squabbling brood,
His wife anchored beside a hill of mending.
Such banal evenings—how they pity him.

By day his food is Plato, Machiavelli,
'Thought is a flower, gentlemen,' he says—
Tracing the thought in air until it grows
Like frost-flowers on the windows of the mind—
'Thought is a flower that has its roots in dung.'
What irony, they think, that one so nourished,
Perfect in all the classic commonwealths,
Himself so signally should lack the arts
To shine and burgeon in the College councils,
A worn-out battery, a nobody, a windbag.
'And yet,' they sigh, 'what has the old boy got,
That every time he talks he fills the hall?'

MRS B

I know—who does not?—Mrs B,
Flushed from the ritual cup of tea.
The cigarette, the symptoms, and the chat,
The black serge skirt and nodding hat—
By these all ladies know
The gallant, tempest-battered crow,
This talkative, good-natured ghoul.

To every Mrs A her Mrs B.
All ladies cool, all ladies fresh and cool
Hear her disreputable story
Of thieving tradesmen, sick relations,
Of suicide by gas, and operations.
She is their grim *memento mori*.

Under the shadow of her trailing skirt
Life's diurnal grease and dirt
Skulk about the kitchen floor.
Every Saturday at nine
She makes, on Doctor Death's front door,
The brass plate and the huge brass knocker shine.
All ladies cool, all ladies cool and mortal—
God keep them far from that conclusive portal.

The Questioning Tiger
1964

EVOLUTION OF A PAINTER

Beneath a pastoral sky, spotted by shadows,
Only by your young, talented eye regarded,
The two farm horses stood, unkempt and useful.
Your heart approved as your deft brush recorded.
One notes the skill; surprised, one notes the love,
And pensive, calm content the scene afforded.

For that was forty years ago, since when
The stoical farm beast has been abolished.
Not so your art, though now the patrons call
For something more expensive and embellished.
Proudly your valuable racers prance
Over the emerald turf, well combed and polished.

We need not twist our mouths with scorn to see
A pretty talent gone corrupt and hard.
Better than you have sold out for champagne.
Enough to know there is, where few regard,
The evidence of your compassion once,
In that ill-lit provincial gallery stored.

COMMAND YOUR DEVIL

Command your devil to lie down and dream.
When he is active, his lascivious eye
Maddens your mind for nothing but the touch
Of furtive hand on hand, thigh against thigh.
All that your wolfish greed contrives will be
A lonely festival of self-disgust,
A murderer's remorse without the blood
The meagre satisfaction of your lust.
So let your devil stalk with you no more
But stay at home and dream. The acts of vice,
The conquests he can fabricate for you
Will your imagination more entice
Than chance encounters quitted with revulsion.
The devil's fantasies use no compulsion.

IMPORTANT INSECTS

Important insects clamber to the top
Of stalks; look round with uninquiring eyes
And find the world incomprehensible;
Then totter back to earth and circumscribe
Irregular territories pointlessly.
Some insects narcisistically assume
Patterns of spots or stripes or burnished sheen
For purposes of sex or camouflage,

Some tweet or rasp, though most are without speech
Except a low, subliminal, mindless chatter.
Take heart: those scientists are wrong who find
Elements of the human in their systems,
Despite their busy, devious trafficking
Important insects simply do not matter.

DE FESCH

For you I search my reference books in vain,
Willem of the impossible name De Fesch.
Vienna was it, Venice, or Amsterdam
Whose plain citizens knew you in the flesh?

Midnight has fallen; the wind unpacified
Moves in the outer darkness while I think
Of that odd sound: not grand, like Palestrina,
Nor quaint, like Dittersdorf or Humperdinck.

Willem de Fesch would seem to be a sound
Not shaped predestinately for high fame;
Nevertheless to-night it pleases me
To celebrate your spirit with your name.

By way of certain pieces for two 'cellos
That spirit earlier breathed upon the air.
Even in an age renowned for melody
Your phrase was of a quality so rare
It spoke out of no time to any time
When a dry heart might wither from despair.

THE SERAPH

Call this your seraph which you seek to kill.
Hugging your inner darkness of despair
In doting arms, you trudge your winter way,
Murdering the snow for its offensive whiteness.
Your well-known shadow is discoursed upon
By anxious German intellectuals;
Less widely recognised, this seraph is
A sort of shadow-self composed of light.
This primal presence, which at home you knew
And trudges with you now through winter streets,
Reverberating in the silent snow,
Is not to be destroyed except one way—
The wilful overfeeding of your shadow.
At night most clearly, while your shadow starves,
Your seraph shines and grows and is your friend.

A STOICAL ROBIN

'A stoical robin solid in the drift'—
I coined the line some seven years ago.
The poem was a failure, but those words
Return to memorise a famous snow.

In fact he wasn't dead. We took him in,
And put him down beside the fire to thaw.
He neither ate our crumbs nor drank our water
But, once revived, true to some primal law,

Took wing and vanished through the open window.
It seemed he'd not accept life as a gift
From those who live in houses, but would rather
Hazard for liberty the frozen drift.

Well, I might follow this excogitation
Into some parable of the human plight.
Instead I conjure from my inner view
A bird whose wings were never spread for flight,

A captive goldfinch chained against a wall.
Was it for pity, anger, or despair
Or simply with a painter's eye for colour
The Dutchman, Carl Fabritius, put him there?

The brilliant plumes are folded, the head firm:
Indifferent or contemptuous, the eyes brood.
A passionless fidelity to nature
Covers the painter's real attitude.

So I may take the chained bird, if I choose,
As emblematic of the mind of man;
And I salute the all-but-unknown artist,
Whether or not this was his conscious plan.

My robin's nothing, but your goldfinch lives,
Becomes an artefact by your success.
Yours lives in freedom, one might say, while mine
Remains imprisoned in my feebleness.

THE BLAMELESS ONE

He, the blameless one, exploring crime
Tried theft and gave the money to the poor;
Slandered and lied and cheated and confessed,
Ran disillusioned from the harlot's door.
Scribbled on walls and washed them clean again
By way of restitution to the city.
Committed arson, called the fire-brigade,
Solicited a cripple from sheer pity.
Finally in a rage of self-reproach
He met an enemy who had been his friend,
Sharpened his knife and followed out of doors,
Thinking 'At last—now I shall make an end.'
The blade struck. Ridiculously the head rolled off.
Appalled, he took the only possible course,
Opened his shirt and drove the knife in hard;
Then woke, shrieking with triumph and remorse.

DISCHARGED FROM HOSPITAL

He stands upon the steps and fronts the morning.
The porter has called a taxi, and behind him
The infirmary doors have swung and come to rest.
Physician, surgeon, and anaesthetist
Have exercised their skill and he is cured.
The rabelaisian sister with the bedpan,
The vigorous masseuse, the sensual nurse
Who washes him modestly beneath a blanket,
The dawn chorus of cleaners, the almoner,
The visiting clergyman—all proceed without him.
He is alone beyond all need of them,
And the saved man goes home, to die of health.

NO TEARS FOR MISS MACASSAR

No tears for Miss Macassar, dispossessed
Three times by an inflexible landlord
Of that small tenement in which she housed
Her ominous, gaunt person and the hoard
Of keepsakes, water-colours, ferns and china.
She and her framed, clerical relations
Now to fresh scenes remove and to new neighbours.
She, stoical connoisseur of all privations,
Treasures her grievances like vintage wine.
So tears for Miss Macassar would be wrong:
She is no miser and too well she knows
Good wine is better shared than kept too long.

DEMIGODS

We demigods can't be too careful, see.
Stricter proprieties hedge us. One slip-up
Can get us a bad name both in heaven and earth.
One of us lies or cheats and some god says
Well, he's half-human—what can you expect?
Another whores or drinks himself to death
And all men vilify his godly vices.
It's hard. But with the gods, how different!

All that they do enhances their prestige,
Or is officially overlooked; or else
Is twisted to adorn the personal legends
They've nothing else to do but manufacture.

Incest or sodomy, it's all the same,
A god must have some respite from his cares.
And erring humans claim divine protection;
But demigods have got to mind their step.

THE HALF–FULL GLASS

I told you I was drained of happiness.
The wine was only half way down our glasses.
You said to me, 'Are you not happy now?'
Searching my heart, I had to own I was.
How should I not be, drinking wine with You?

'Whatever dies was not mixed equally,'
Donne said. If so, love is without death,
For half the happiness of meeting you
Is pain at knowing we must separate;
And therefore love can never be complete.
A glass untasted, and an empty glass,
Are nothing but mere hope and memory.
The glass in which I drink your health contains
Now and always half emptiness, half wine.

RAINLESS

Roots in the darkened garden drink the rain
Where in the sun we walked some hours ago.
My need, no less than theirs, unguessed by you,
To take you in my arms and perpetrate
An undeclaring and forbidden love
Revives in me what was a habit once.
It is endurable—as is the thought
There is no problem where is no solution.
So, like a statue that no kiss evokes,
You to my inner eye make manifest,
Recall that sculptors turn their love to stone
Creating flesh beyond the reach of passion.
Then let the garden drink its fill; my roots
Need no one's pity, least of all my own.

GENERATION OF A CRITIC

The eager eye that went with you to school
Reported birds' eggs in the thicket;
The heart your mother and your father split
Was healed by girls and village cricket.

The euphuistic tongue and pen you practised
To gain no other recognition
Than that boon friend's you walked or drank beside.
Then Satan told you of ambition.

He whispered fame, wealth, power—and all that;
He promised honorary degrees;
He told you no one ever made a name
By cutting other names in trees.

So now the eager eye that went to school
With jealousy has gone a-squint;
The tongue is shrill, the ink turned poison,
Getting and keeping you in print.

BRUGES

And here, in the tiny city of the unloved,
Every third shop-window is a confectioner's,
In which daily on their walk from work
The mundane inhabitants eat heaven with their eyes.
That other heaven to which their faith consigns them
Is meanwhile populated only by sugar-angels
And the notes of bells
Breaking quarter-hourly from sky-high stone
      imprisonment
Like birds on scattered crumbs.
So lives the generation of the hungry
In a city piled with sweetmeats.

THE TIGER

They have sat in their wide window and approved
Irregularities of the autumn sky
Between the coasts of the sycamore and yew.
They have banished the questioning tiger from their
      land
Who might have resurrected the old fear
Springing like joy in the striped glades of childhood.
They have long known that the pursuing beasts
That strike at them on waking are themselves,
Have ceased to love the tiger for his hate.

JAMES SON AND SPICER

We specialise in disordered consciences.
'You owe—we know' is our motto.
We assure you of close attention at all times.
Signed, for James Son and Spicer, Squiggle.
The seven-and-sixpence due to the landlady,
The good turn you might have done a friend,
The photographs you borrowed and retained,
We, James Son and Spicer,
Of everywhere in particular, know.
If you blame your own inadequacies on the hydrogen
    bomb,
Or sneak off in fantasy
To the Ruby Joy School of Ballroom Dancing
(Partners provided), we know.
If not, we find out. Nothing
Is overlooked, mislaid, or put into the wrong file.

People attending interviews for promotion,
Women writers composing reminiscences,
Men climbing ladders,
Men passing between coaches on moving trains,
Men with eccentric neckties,
Or consciously illegible signatures,
James Son and Spicer takes care of them all.
They are the special province
Of our Evasions and Half-truths Department.

A word from us in the right quarter
Can ensure, or frustrate, an O.B.E.,
C.B.E., D.B.E.,
Ph.D., B.Sc. or other degree.
Our contacts are universal and sufficient.

James Son and Spicer's records are
Complete, discreet, up-to-the-minute,
Self-deleting in case of theft or unauthorised perusal.
Our confidential dossiers are second to none.
James Son and Spicer's registered address
Is a mere blind. Telegraphic communications
To 'Slips, Paternoster' will not reach us.
But an ad in *The Times* personal column
Or a small card in your window with our initials
Will bring an accredited agent to your door,
In plain clothes, plain-spoken, clean-shaven.
You may not like him.
But do not try anything. He is fully covered.
Our business code is tough but ethical.
Your mistake is our opportunity.
James Son and Spicer put the T in Terror.

TRADITIONAL

Strenuously downstream with muscles flexed,
See how he manages his sleek canoe.
All on the banks appraise
The style, the masterful technique, the resolute gaze.
'There is a man who will,' they say, 'arrive.'
Down the main stream, dead centre, see him strive.
We in our slothful punts keep to the shallows.
We hug the bank and watch the moorhens ride.
No trophy and no race
Seduce us from our talk and this unhurried pace.
May all such muscular candidates prefer
The main stream, leaving us the backwater.

SPICER'S INSTANT POETRY

On sale everywhere: Spicer's Instant Poetry.
Trial size, 2/-; epic pack, 19/6.
A balanced mixture of clichés, catchwords,
Symbols, non sequiturs, ambiguities,
Stock phrases and borrowings from the best models.
Warranted free from superfluous emotion,
Bad rhymes and obvious plagiarism.
Simply add luke-warm milk and water.
A child can use it.
One teaspoonful reconstitutes a sonnet.
This infallible preparation
Makes poems suitable for competitions,
National and international festivals,
Private greetings cards and autograph albums.
Results guaranteed, and are to be seen
In best literary journals.
Spicer's Instant Poetry comes in seven popular
    shades:
Nature (including animals), childhood, domestic
    troubles,
Industry and politics, thwarted love,
Mythology and religion, foreign parts.
Special 'Parnassus' kit containing all the above
    varieties,
Free surprise item and coloured art portrait of leading
    bard,
Or 'Tartan Special' for Scottish subjects,
Five shillings only, post free.
Extra strong mix for homosexual or surgical pieces.
Delighted user writes: 'Instant Poetry

Is a joy for ever . . . Indistinguishable from the real
     thing.'
Order now and astonish your friends.
Big cash opportunities: Immortality
Assured or money returned.

A KIND OF LOVE

You wait, it seems, upon the edge of sunlight
As if you said 'There'll be a shower perhaps'.
'Perhaps a storm,' I say, and had I power
As fear creeps down
Over the darkening pasture
To guarantee the sunshine, you should walk
Free there, and saved. But since I cannot change
Or even share the weather where you live,
Call weather-wisdom ineffectual
That does not tell itself: not of my world
The sunshine where assuredly you shall walk.
To learn impossibility from you
Is to be reconciled ungrudgingly
To yet another of the kinds of love,
The kind of love by which the loser wins.

PLANNING PERMISSION

He looked at me without surprise or pleasure
But with a bored, habitual compassion.
'They sent me here,' I said. 'I want to build.'
'Naturally,' he said. 'We'll see what we can do.'
Along the hopeless counter twenty others
Were seeing what they could do.
                              'You'll need these forms.'
Application for permission for an erection
For occupation as residential accommodation
And/or private domestic habitation.
'In triplicate of course. Return when filled
To the assistant sub-divisional officer.'
I took the papers. Tears of gratitude
Misted my sight; but he was gone already
Into the wastes beneath his sandy hair.

I took the papers back.
Alone in his little room
The assistant sub-divisional officer sent for me.
He looked at me without surprise or pleasure
But with compassionate unrecognition.
'Permission for an erection. Quite so. We'll write.'
'Oh thank you, sir,' I started. 'Do you think . . .?'
But under the sandy hair the eyes were blank.
After eleven months the answer came.
'Rejection of permission for an erection.
Any appeal to be directed within three years
To the sub-divisional officer for attention.'

Two years and more went by before I gained
The sub-divisional officer's section. With relief
I saw that he at least had had his due reward.

Between the flat ears under the greying hair
No sign of recognition stirred.
                              'Ah yes.
Objection to rejection of application for erection.'
With the old bored compassion in his voice,
'We'll do,' he promised, 'what we can to help.'
'Oh sir,' I sobbed. He interrupted me.
'I'll pass on your objection to the divisional officer.
It may take time.'
                    Re-charged with hope I went.

I died; and here I falter by the gate
Drained of desire and too ashamed to face
The sorrowing figure on the throne of grace.

IT WOULD BE WRONG

It would be wrong to say
The dead lack all regard.
I note, whichever way I turn,
Their strange solicitude.

To care as the dead care
Is to be coldly kind
And strictly fair.

If in a statue's head
The eyes are wholly blind,
Then why avoid their gaze
And shiver as you pass?

And if the books you stare at
Are uncompassionate,
Why try to not offend
Their letter and their spirit?

A noble building stands
Insentient, you would say,
And yet controls our thoughts
By stating order.

Let us care as the dead care,
Dispassionate;
See as they see, unmoved;
Speak as they speak,
Slowly, not for effect,
Without frivolity,
Truthfully,
Since none can answer us.

POOR WOMAN

She backed him for a win
In the Immortality Stakes.
Here, she thought, is someone
Who amounts to something
Or something which amounts
To someone.
For fifty mortal years
She has endured his vanity,
Duplicity, boorishness, insensitivity—
And what is her reward?
Tired, harassed and grey,
As the mourners go, she says:
To hell with immortality. Thank God that's over.
Her own immortal lot she has endured daily
For fifty years, is now
Heartily sick of it.

IMPROVISATIONS

1

PLASTIC

This popular wreath, the plastic model,
    Which only the vulgar-hearted crave,
Will last when every swollen noddle
    That wears it will be in the grave.
Yet who'd preserve a thing so cheap,
    So dearly bought at any cost?
Its place is on the rubbish heap:
    True fame is neither sought nor lost.

2

BE CERTAIN, MR A—Z

Be Certain, Mr A to Z,
    That when the vulture drops its dirt
Upon your undistinguished head
    It is not chance but your desert.

3

TO BE IS LOVE

To be, and not to think, is love:
So while I love you, love, I am,
Not less because I prize the light
More than the heat of this live flame.
Irrational love is like the bird
That serenades the setting sun
And sings upon the orchard top
Despite the farmer and his gun.

PRECEPT

Dwell in some decent corner of your being,
Where plates are orderly set and talk is quiet,
Not in its devious crooked corridors
Nor in its halls of riot.

5

THINGS TO COME

The shadow of a fat man in the moonlight
  Precedes me on the road down which I go;
And should I turn and run, he would pursue me:
  This is the man whom I must get to know.

CONVERTING THE VICARAGE

His was a comely residence, though crumbling.
  His ghost in a flurry of surplice has pattered away.
You the new owners will have much to look to
    Before you come to stay.

Re-point the brickwork and expel the damp;
  Renew the guttering; repair the stair;
Replace broken panes; strengthen the chimneys;
    But especially, and everywhere

In every corner you will have to reckon with
  A multifarious, sub-human population
Living in garret, gable, cupboard and corridor
    By gradual usurpation.

Mild-eyed, irascible, tyrannous or fussy,
  Conventional, stupid, active or plumb lazy,
They live deviously, act enviously,
    And can drive you crazy.

Proof against exorcism, they cannot be smoked out,
  Gassed out, thrown out by force or charm.
Better to give them *de facto* recognition—
    In fact they mean you no harm.

True, they will try to regulate your lives.
  If you reasonably protest, they won't heed you.
You will be made to feel you live by their leave.
    But consider: they need you.

They need your food and drink to batten on;
  They need your heat and your vitality;
And since they've nothing but their self-importance
    They need your pity.

So, though you may not rid your house of them,
  In course of time perhaps you'll make them see
That while they meanly live as parasites
    You are, in spirit, free.

INDIRECT SPEECH

Schoolmasters regularly fulminate
Against the horrors of official jargon;
And yet if these reformers had their way
I'm not so sure we'd get a better bargain.

Although admittedly periphrasis
Imparts an air of unreality,
Under the circumstances now obtaining
It might be better to let evil be.

To-day I had a buff, official notice
Couched in the smoothest, most obsequious terms;
But what it meant was: 'We can break you, Reeves;
You'd better pay up quick, you worm of worms!'

GOAT AND COMPASSES

By etymologies of public houses
Many are tempted to rash speculation.
This 'Goat and Compasses', where now we tend,
Must surely have a likelier derivation
Than 'God encompasseth us'—such irony
Could any mind unprejudiced admit?
Step to the bar and order what you will,
And in our private angle as we sit
These compasses can signify the force
That holds our thoughts within the civil order;
The goat obscenely leads them in a dance
Up to the outlaw country on the border.
The anarchic goat and rational compasses,
These are the warring standards that divide:
But here in conference in our private angle
Under this sign our thoughts are pacified.

THE SOLVERS

Invalids and other hotel residents
Unpuzzle themselves with patience-cards and
   jigsaws.
Crosswords engage saloon passengers at sea.
Philosophers invent puzzles with answers.
Each knows that what he is trying *can* be done.
Not all enjoy such comfort of assurance.
I, watching the backs of houses and of books,
Work away at my mind, fitting the pieces,
Pairing the cards, rejecting words.
So sitting, I become suddenly conscious
Of playing patience with crooked pieces,
While solving an incomplete jigsaw with words
In the precise non-language of a dream.
Some of the pieces fit, some of the cards match,
Only some of the pieces and the cards are lost.
I have tried to play it according to the rules,
Only the rules they sent are in Chinese.
Is it too late, I ask, to start again?
Or will extinction, when it comes, surprise me
Sorting the pieces, working out the clues?

GRAND OPERA

The lovers have poisoned themselves and died singing,
And the crushed peasant father howls in vain.
For his duplicity, lubricity and greed
The unspeakable base count is horribly slain.

After the music, after the applause,
The lights go up, the final curtain drops.
The clerks troop from the house, and some are
      thinking:
Why is life different when the singing stops?

All that hysteria and those histrionics,
All those coincidences were absurd.
But if there were no relevance to life,
Why were they moved to shudder and applaud?

Though they outlived that passion, it was theirs,
As was the jealousy, the sense of wrong
When some proud jack-in-office trampled them;
Only it did not goad them into song.

The accidents, the gross misunderstandings,
Paternal sorrow, amorous frustration
Have they not suffered? Was the melodrama
An altogether baseless imitation?

Subsong
1969

NOTE

I owe the title of this volume to Mr D. W. Snow, who has kindly allowed me to quote, by way of explanation, from his beautiful book, *A Study of Blackbirds* (Allen and Unwin, 1958, to whom also grateful acknowledgments are made). Subsong, Mr Snow writes, differs chiefly from subdued song and full autumn song 'in being much quieter, only audible a few yards away, and delivered with the beak closed and throat barely moving. I have recorded subsong,' he continues, 'from both old and young males from August right through the winter, but most often from young birds on fine days in October and November. It seems to have no function with respect to other birds, and, as Gurr says, to be given "for the sole benefit of the performer". Not only is it audible for only a short distance, but it has a certain ventriloquial quality and is frequently given from thick cover, so that the singer, though only a few feet away, is often very difficult to locate. Birds also give subsong while foraging among leaf litter on the ground, only interrupting it when they suddenly dig for a morsel of food. A modified form of subsong is sometimes given during display. Often when courting, and less often when engaged in intense threat displays with an equally matched rival, males utter a subdued version of the song, hurried and confused and strongly giving the impression that the bird is prevented from singing normally by being strangled.'

ALL DAYS BUT ONE

All days but one shall see us wake to make
Our last confession:
Bird notes at dawn revive the night's obsession.

In this dark light I need not see to be
My own confessor:
Crime still is crime, the greater and the lesser.

There is no calculus we know can show,
No sum can prove,
Love that is three parts guilt is one part love.

We conjure from some inner place the face,
Perhaps the voice
On which we fix what we must call our choice.

Not these console us, but some word we heard
Or thought we heard
When doubts awake us with the waking bird.

The saving word of love we thought we caught
Might have redeemed,
Could we be certain it was said, not dreamed.

But when the love we would have built on guilt
Is mere illusion,
Bird notes at dawn repeat the night's confusion.

THE DOUBLE AUTUMN

Better to close the book and say good-night
When nothing moves you much but your own plight.
Neither the owl's noise through the dying grove
Where the small creatures insecurely move,
Nor what the moon does to the huddled trees,
Nor the admission that such things as these
Would have excited once can now excite.
Better close down the double autumn night
Than practise dumbly staring at your plight.

THIS CORRUPT MUSIC

This corrupt music of the violin—
Its consolations fail the inveterate ear,
Satiate with formal, timeless eloquence.
He groans to be relieved from absolute beauty
By the warm impact of ephemeral life.
The music flesh extracts from naked flesh,
Unheard and unrecorded, needs no score.

Only the fully lived can fully die.
What the inveterate ear supposes lived
Fell short of life. The unconsoling phrase
Speaks what it never knew, corrupt in beauty;
What never lived lives now in its corruption.
Death is the silent tune flesh plays on flesh.

FINALITIES

Some things are final. Whether love fail or prosper
In the loved presence scarcely seems to count.
All hopes, permissions, possibilities
Are mere irrelevance. These are of time.
Absence and separation are of time,
Are time. Presence is final and sufficient.
Hope is the fantasy conceived of absence;
Present, I look at you in pure despair.

I spend my life, like others, asking questions
That are no questions since they have no answer.
This is a practice taught us by the Greeks.
So now the question that I ask is this:
Why is it that for forty years and more
A certain cast of face, a certain aspect
Has always been to me classic and final?
I see a brow and nose, a mouth and eyes,
A bone-shape that subtends a mask of flesh;
Know that, before I saw, I knew and loved;
Experience the chill of death that comes
From every intimation of perfection
Breathed from a polar field of ultimate snow.

To long to hold the unpossessable,
To long to kiss the unapproachable
Is violating snow to look for warmth.

A SONG FOR LOVERS

We lay beside the dying fire.
There was no light but what it gave.
We saw each burning particle
Fall unresisting to its grave.

We had not known each other long,
Yet I believe our late-born love
Was co-extensive with the life
That breathed within the fiery grove.

You said, 'A million winters past
A robin whistled on the bough
That dies to keep our bodies warm,
And his the song that cheers us now.'

SONG

The sleep I lost for you last night
I might have found at break of day
Had not the lapidary birds
These waking words conspired to say:

The only hell is guilt unshared;
A silence shared need not be broken.
The worst of love is not to speak;
The best of love is never spoken.

THE SIGNED PAGE

Blood from my flayed heart, sticky on my hands,
Is signature on every page I write.
'Serenity and turbulence' must be
The epigraph to every hard-wrought volume—
Serenity the only prize I sought,
And turbulence my final only lot.

NOCTURNAL

To passers in the moon-white square
The newest statue made as if to say
'Listen—listen', but his frozen breath
Hurried them on their way;
His sightless monumental stare
Reminded lovers of the look of death,
An impulse on the hard nocturnal air,
The appealing gesture failed,
Secret and ineffectual as despair.
'Be still, be still,' muttered the others then,
'Be as we are, the wind-worn and the old.
Accustomed to our self-begotten cold,
We unremarked outwear the lives of men.'

THE GRACELESS BANQUET

For what we have not received the Lord make us
    shameful
Is grace for such a meal,
The graceless banquet of humiliation.
Breaking stones for blood
Is asking sympathy of a narcissist.
That immature wine is sour. When the belly-ache
Convicts us of emotional greed
Self-blame's the bone given us to chew on.
After such fare the usual prescription,
Death's way to health, abstention and despair.

THE SHIPMAN IN THE BLOOD

The shipman in his blood goes buffeting
Pulled by unfathomable currents where
The bibulous landsmen neither know nor care,
Giving and getting mockery and drink.
Before and after, in a night of ink,
He craves their charted, mercenary lives
Who have not spied the seagull on his mast
Nor understood what man and bird have guessed—
The shipman in the blood enjoys no rest
Between his mother's and the ocean's breast.

METAMORPHOSIS

You found, by small hours of your running feet,
The coastal waters sliding, insect wings,
And voices multifarious amid leaves,
Not knowing then
The territories of your big desire
By time's enormity would turn
To little wicked areas of flesh;
And now when feet are slow,
Dawn birds mere carrion
The alps and thickets of the needed body
Are inaccessible as voices speaking
Across the rise and fall of classic fountains.
What would the senses give, you ask, for such
An instant context for their morning play,
A warm and actual territory in flesh?

THE MEETING

There was a meeting.
No one was in charge of the meeting.
Someone said 'We need more conscious control.'
'No, less.'
I felt contentious but said little.
There was no music or flowers, and the colour of the
    meeting was brown.
Neil lay with his head on the floor.
Under it was my jacket, rolled up.
I removed the jacket and put a waste-paper basket
    over his head.
There was a meeting.
Someone said that something I had said
Was very reasonable.
'If Franz had not lived, it would be necessary to
    invent him.'
I handed my daughter a cake a friend had brought.
She said it was useless and she had brought a bigger one.
There was a meeting.
Beryl came and said to me 'Can you manage a canoe?'
I said 'Yes'.
She said 'Oh good!' radiantly. 'Then you can take us
    all out
On the Regent's Canal.'
We made no progress.
Somebody paid me a dull compliment.
Someone said 'There is news from the Kingdom of
    Nails'.
One or two were reading books.
Franz . . . or was it 'France'?
In dreams there is no boredom.

'We need to widen the spectrum of communication.'
'Here is a poem,' said Geoffrey, standing up with an
    open book in his hand,
'Which I think will move right into the language.'

No one was listening, and he did not read.
Another said 'Everything I have not willed is boring'
    and left the room abruptly.
Stephen said
'Every concern gets the Ian Hamilton it deserves.'
You can know in a dream that you are dreaming
But outside a dream you can never be certain you are
    not.

TO NOT LOVE

One looked at life in the prince style, shunning pain.
Now one has seen too much not to fear more.
Apprehensive, it seems, for all one loves,
One asks only to not love, to not love.

A SONATA BY HANDEL

I cranked my clockwork gramophone;
The music told me I should never tire
To hear its timeless tone.
It did not tell me and I did not care
What else might chance.
Older by thirty years and more,
I hear a different fiddle dance
And different fingers press the keys
To that consummate score.
All that was seen and unforeseen—
Wife, children, sickness, death and war,
The headlines of the time between—
Whatever it has taught, has taught me nothing
More than I knew before
Of that slow, rapid, rueful and euphoric dance
The periwigged blind German first performed
Than that it once was right, is right, and will be right
Whenever sounds excite
Whatever mind, whatever years elapse:
Such music is a view of life perhaps?

FACES AT THE BRINK

Suppose, against the darkness of your mind
Just at the brink of sleep you see, as I do,
Faces and forms of people glittering small:
Malignant, threatening, or merely odd
And always enigmatic, always strangers.
What is the sense and origin, you ask,
Of such involuntary apparitions?
They lurk, they question, they accuse, they smile;
And I believe that they are those we saw
Subliminally once on crowded pavements,
In theatres, railways stations, hotel bars.
The brain must register and store these masks,
Project them as we near the brink of sleep
To disconcert and vex us as we plunge.
So if a visage angular and hard
Glares at you through myopic spectacles,
Square-jawed, brow furrowed, mouth severe and chill,
Or twisted in a thin, ironic smile,
Trying to speak, trying to comprehend—
Then to your inner dark let no such visage
Add panic or despair: consider rather
That somewhere once your path converged with mine;
And that, over that gulf of unacquaintance,
I come to wish you nothing worse than sleep.

NO STRAWBERRIES FROM
MR WRIGHT

On New Year's Day the New Year Honours find
No loyal Briton quite indifferent.
This one at last, we note, has got his K;
That one must face, we read with satisfaction,
The disappointment of an M.B.E.—
Winners at the nation's prizegiving.
You and I, of course, have ceased to meditate
For many years, even in fantasy,
The dignified letter of refusal . . .
                              This year
My thoughts revert to Mr Wright.
Him, paragon of schoolmasters forty years back,
I hear preside over the History test,
Staccato and terrific,
The praise, the blame, the rich compulsory jokes;
Or on the draughty field nursing the bowling
For the big game; or on Sunday evenings
In the brown schoolroom, while the daylight died,
Great in his chair with *David Blaize*.
                              Each June
Brought strawberry time and Mr Wright's birthday.
I see them now, prefects, pubescent cricketers,
The paragon's inner circle seated round him
At the top table, eager and superb.
Munificent at the head sits Mr Wright
Distributing the fruit, the cream, the sugar.
These special benefactions done,
The royal eye roams down the dining-room
To where the undistinguished lower orders
Feed prosily on thick bread and grey tea.

The eye detects a favoured commoner.
'Ah, Parkhouse, you don't care for strawberries? . . .
You do?' The voice of conscious bounty beckons.
'Then bring your plate up.' Then another
And another gets the cherished birthday honour,
And Mr Wright is Bacchus at the board.
I never was so favoured. I wore specs,
Had an unhealthy interest in books,
And was suspected (wrongly as it happened)
Of having cheated in the sports. At twelve
I bore no malice. Philosophically
I accepted the royal will. It was my fault.
I did not hate strawberries, or Mr Wright;
I did not even hate my friends.
                                    And so
I wonder what has chanced in forty years
To make me hate buyers of birthday love,
And why to me all Mr Wrights are wrong.

JACOBEAN

Lolling too long in elegant lean hose,
Unmarked the sensual pages drift away.
The nuncios' urgent bombast is mere pose.
The waiting women are inclined to play.
And so within the anterooms of state
The great seem small, the small are nearly great.

YOU READ TOO MUCH

You read too much; you hear too much perhaps.
My over-anxious friend, you need no book
To understand the writing in the clouds.
Next week the clouds may have a better look.

Never be less than fair to medallists,
Since to much worse you have been more than kind.
Dig well your orchard, and anticipate
A little of the fortune you will find.

When apples swell beneath a warmer sky,
It shall be written there for you to see:
'Not all the kings have little wicked beards,
Not every general drinks blood for tea.'

YOU AND NOT YOU

Practise the furtive eye, the mean excuse,
The casual voice that hides the anxious lie;
Pretend to cynicism, wear a beard,
Reject all fair advances with abuse.

Then none but your true friends will recognise,
If friend remain, the decent man at last,
When newly shaven, self-revealed and free,
You stand to greet the day of undisguise.

PERSONALITY CULT

Instructions by a Celebrity for his Posthumous Radio Portrait

When I am very dead, remember me,
But not the real me: leave that alone.
Call on the raddled dowager in Venice
And prop her up before a microphone.
My tamest jokes, most threadbare platitudes
She will retail in clichés all her own:
Then let the old bar bore pontificate
About my 'characteristic attitudes'.
Exhume the gardener; he will proudly boast
Of how I spoke to him as to a gent.
Let the world know how much my friendship meant
To the quack writer whom I hated most.
But above all, the ghosts of hostesses
At Georgian weekends, long in tooth and claw,
In tones as flat as oriental prints
Must quaveringly tell how on their lawns
In Berkshire, or amidst the Chelsea chintz,
I chatted literature with Bonar Law.
Say I was kind to animals and tradesmen;
Say how I lisped, and how my back-hair curled;
But do not say in Gath and Askelon
You bored me once and now you bore the world.
When I am very dead, remember me;
Let anything be told except the truth.
They didn't know me; I was no one's poodle
Vice made me man in age and fear in youth.

POETRY FESTIVAL

Wrapped in my enigmatic small cigar
I register the world of noise
Where every poet is a megaphone
Which shouts immortal megaphone.
Trumpet narcissus is a flower
Of which the simple message is itself
And trifling indications show
It does not have the trick of human love.
The inventor's scientific care
Could if it would provide the antidote,
Patent a small effectual cigar
To emanate a soundproof smoke.

ON TWO POETS

*competing with each other as to which preaches in the
more churches.*

Mistrust, young man, the protestants of your age,
Rebels beneath the banners of dissent:
You'll live to see them man no barricades
But climb the pulpits of the establishment.

SOJOURNERS IN THE DESERT

To live on fantasy as I did—that was to live on sand.
I stumbled onward mouthing dust, stung by the wind
    to blindness.
'Sojourners in the desert know the accidents of
    bounty'—
Thus Lawrence of Arabia writes of some unlooked for
    kindness.

What compensation sends me now, almost
    unbearably,
Groping about this pathless time as in a nightmare
    county,
Your trust, your need, your actual touch, your young
    and warm compassion?
Sojourners in the desert know the accidents of
    bounty.

Poems and Paraphrases
1972

ROUGH WEATHER

To share with you this rough, divisive weather
And not to grieve because we have to share it,
Desire to wear the dark of night together
And feel no colder that we do not wear it,
Because sometimes my sight of you is clearer,
The memory not clouded by the sense,
To know that nothing now can make you dearer
Than does the close touch of intelligence,
To be the prisoner of your kindnesses
And tell myself I want you to be free,
To wish you here with me despite all this,
To wish you here, knowing you cannot be—
This is a way of love in our rough season,
This side of madness, the other side of reason.

THE SPARK

If, as you read, you sigh and yawn,
Remember, I am one who talks
And thinks and writes and does not live.
So if I say I live in you,
Do not retort I overstate:
I reverence him, I warm to her,
I love them but they do not feed
The fire by which I almost live.

The fire by which I almost live
Was once a blaze, is now a spark,
So if you sigh and yawn, that spark
Will glow the more because you breathe.

NOT TO BE GREEDY

Not to be greedy for you, not to hoard you;
Not to begrudge you others to whom also
You have much to give;
Not to repine at absence, imagine neglect;
Not to be jealous, envious; still less to gorge
On the self-loving sweets of gratitude,
The masochistic bread of self-abasement,
The secret hope that you will never be free,
Despite the freedom freely exchanged between us—
All this is hard. To be an ideal
Is to be hard. To be hard is an ideal.

LATE LOVE

If of this man you know the history,
Secret and innermost, then you know well
That of the four loves of his proper being
Yours is the latest and perhaps the last.
Sounds we are born to and survive our age
Are those the wind makes, blowing round the world,
To which we add 'I want, I wish, I love'.
We give the cosmic breath significance.

SEPTEMBER DUSK

The girl and the five boys have gone with their
    burden of apples,
A tangle of bright clothes and disputation.
Darkness spreads from under the leaves of the fig-tree,
The brown nut-tree and the bramble thicket.
The territorial birds have stationed themselves
    for the night;
Some talk—none sings. There can be too much
     silence,
And too much certainty, as that your light tread
Will not disturb this gloom, your voice this silence.
In mockery perhaps it might be asking
'What is a thousand miles to one who hears?'
And I might answer,
    'Simplest things are hardest to accept.
Distance is simple. Causes of grief are many,
    but all simple.'
Children and birds have closed the book of day,
But I shall turn the pages of the night
Lying with my erosive enemy
Far from the echo of a voice, a footfall.

MESSAGE

Be absolute for poetry, my friend,
Or your insatiate spirit will go hungry,
Knocking on deaf men's doors to ask for bread.
Who has the saving word will never starve.
There was a wave of bitterness on which
I swam ashore. Naked, companionless,
I had exactly life and nothing more.
The fates gave us a choice of this or that.
There is no bargaining. It was either death
Or life upon this salty element,
Banged from one desperate corner to the next,
The taste of salt for ever on my tongue.

CLOISTERED

Let us not visualise the shapes of love
Nor the demure tonality of features
But reason of the archetypal dove,
The special iconography of creatures,
So to alleviate our minds' despair
By riddling out the symbols of the air.
Pictorial brotherhoods contrive to see
The Holy Ghost as ornithology.

THE CHILDREN

These pretty children with their reading eyes
Distract you from the journey and the prize.
It is a chaste, an innocent distraction;
Of you they make this innocent exaction,
That you take note of them, and smile, and look,
And be at once their mirror and their book.
They need it so, and you desire it so;
And through your voice in time they come to know
The essential difference of their condition,
Demanding as their right its recognition.
The courting tone is now their expectation,
Monarch and subject each in his own station.
And if they harden, they will feel no shame;
For their corruption you must take the blame.
Their watching eyes will read, as due, your guilt,
On which, and not on their mere pride, is built
The boundless bounty of their self-regard.
Necessities of self-defence are hard.
Pursue the journey; suffer to be wise,
And win the loser's consolation prize.

SONG

Suffer these hands, the heart's interpretation.
Because I come to you as one who comes
Not at the minute's nor the mind's dictation,
Suffer these hands, the heart's interpretation.

                                                    1930

YOU TOO WILL LEARN TO CRY

You too will learn to cry when you are older
And know there is no gain in holding back.
The rigid mouth, poised eyebrow and straight
        shoulder
Are tokens, not of fullness, but of lack.

The scalding tears of infants rolling down
Express the plenitude of sheer despair:
You realise by them that rainstorms drown
Acres of drought, and tempests cool the air.

PROUD WALKERS

See the proud walkers toss
Their curled, magnificent hair,
Vain in a world of loss
And a polluted air.

And age can give you nothing
Except a taste for death,
The sourness of self-loathing,
Truth on the final breath.

FIN DE SAISON

Much of my life—how much?—has been transacted
At café counters on the sunny streets:
But now evening descends, the leaves descend,
And yawning waiters hurry on my death.
It is ordained no man shall have for long
The faculty of self-regeneration,
So with a syllable of leave-taking,
A final tip, I drift into the night.
Next week the cafés close for renovation.

ANIMULA

No one knows, no one cares—
An old soul
In a narrow cottage,
A parlour,
A kitchen,
And upstairs
A narrow bedroom,
A narrow bed—
A particle of immemorial life.

A QUESTION

Adrift in the polluted garden, ask:
The uninhibiting draught, the hands' entreaty,
The night's avowal and the morning's penance—
Is there no different course, no other sequence?

BAGATELLES

WHEN TWO

When two have no nutrition but the air
Love is the product of a twin despair.

EUPHORIA

The exaltation of the evening comes
When to their graves the tired members fall.
Is there no stratagem by which to save
This mood of exaltation for us all?

TO HELP US

Technology has found no way
To help us, in our desperation,
Build on the ruin of a day
An evening's reconciliation.

IN LESS THAN SECONDS

I look into their beautiful passing faces.
In less than seconds worlds have swum apart.

ROBERTO GERHARD'S FOURTH SYMPHONY

A strong noise hits the amber air,
The ambient air about my chair;
By which I know there is an affirmation
Of what you might call neo-civilisation.

A VOICE

How badly and how beautifully she speaks.
Her voice is like a Sunday evening chime,
As stupid and evocative as her face,
Moving and childish as an ancient rhyme.

A MYSTERY

Some necessary jottings of my trade
I noted lately on a tape-recorder
Today, a fortnight after, when replayed
Revealed a message of a different order . . .

ONE PROPRIETY

There's only one propriety
(Whatever you may think)—
To nurture in sobriety
The brats we get in drink.

ACT OF MERCY

The deaf, blind cripple shuffled on,
Was cornered by the corner-lurkers,
Gave no resistance, groaned and died—
And cheated all the welfare-workers.

VARIATION ON A CLICHÉ

She stood you up, she let you down,
She smashed your pride, the red red rose;
So now in disarray you stand,
A carving knife in your right hand
And in your left a severed nose.

ETHOLOGY

When the geese write a book
On Konrad Lorenz,
Ethology
Will begin to make sense.

MOMENTS IN HELL

[from Dante's *Inferno*]

O blind cupidity, evil and foolish,
Which in this short life is our great incentive
And proves our ruin in the life to come . . .

Help me, good Vulcan, help your master, Jove,
In Mongibello at the black forge crying.

Here there was less than night and less than day,
So that my vision went not far before,
But in my ears I felt a high horn sounding.

This I have spoken so that thou mayst suffer.

I, Master Adam, coiner when alive,
Had everything I might desire, and now
Sighing I crave a single drop of water.

The third of these translations was given in the original as an Epigraph to my last collection:

Quivi era men che notte e men che giorno
Si che il viso m'andava innanzi poco;
Ma io senti' sonare un alto corno.

SPLEEN

[after *Spleen* by Charles Baudelaire]

I am the prince of a rain-sodden kingdom,
Rich and yet powerless, young and very old;
The curtseys of my mentors I disdain,
And pass the time in boredom with my dogs,
In hunting and in hawking take no pleasure
Nor in my people starving at the gates.
The drollest ballad of my favourite jester
Excites no laughter in this harsh, sick prince.
My bed, powdered with lilies, is a tomb.
The ladies of the chamber think me handsome
But can contrive no costume so indecent
As to regale this youthful skeleton.
The man of science with his potable gold
Has never purged my body of corruption,
And in those blood-baths we derive from Rome,
Remembered in old age by men of power,
I have not learned to warm my sluggish corpse
Where green Lethean water flows, not blood.

TWILIGHT

[after *Le Crépuscule du Soir* by Charles Baudelaire]

See where delightful evening, friend of the crook,
Partner in crime, comes with his wolf tread.
Like a huge alcove slowly the sky shuts.
Men cannot wait to change into wild beasts.

Evening, dear evening, haven of him whose arms
Can truly tell him 'We have worked today',
Of him whose heart is crushed by savage grief,
The dogged scholar with the brow of lead
And the bowed labourer trudging home to sleep.
Meanwhile the unwholesome demons of the air
Wake heavily like business men, take wing
And bang themselves on gables and on shutters.
Then gaudy prostitution in the streets
Begins to flaunt beneath the flapping lights,
Issues from ant-hill apertures, marks out
Ubiquitous secret tracks, as one who plots
A sudden ambush. Like a ravening worm
It gnaws the breast of the polluted city.

You hear on every side the hiss of kitchens,
The squeaking theatres and snorting bands,
Those gambling-hells, the sleazy restaurants
Fill up with tarts and their accomplice sharks.
Thieves too, who work without respite or pity,
Pry open doors and safes with gentle fingers,
To eat for a few days and trick out their whores.

At this climactic hour let me withdraw
And still the clamour. Is it not the time

That sharpens all the anguish of the sick?
The stranglehold of night is on their necks.
They near their journey's end and move towards
The common pit; their sighing fills the poorhouse.
Some never more at dusk will know again
The chimney corner and the fragrant soup
Beside a loved companion. All their lives
Some have not known the warmth and tenderness
Of their own fireside. They have never lived.

SIR PERCIVALE

[after *Parsifal* by Paul Verlaine]

Sir Percivale has overcome the girls,
Their pleasant chatter and diverting lust;
Has overcome his virgin boy's desire
For their small breasts and their diverting chatter,
Has overcome the subtle-hearted beauty
Displaying her cool arms and sensual throat,
Has conquered Hell, returning to his tent
His boy's arm weighted with a heavy trophy,
That spear with which the sacred flank was pierced;
He has healed the King: now he is King himself,
Priest of the quintessential, holiest treasure;
As glory and symbol, in a golden robe,
Adores the chalice with the real blood—
And O those children chanting in the choir!

THE ALBATROSS

[after *L'Albatros* by Charles Baudelaire]

Sometimes the idle seamen take
That huge seabird the albatross
Who, indolent fellow-voyager,
Pursues them in their salty wake.

This king who in the blue sky soars
Is lowered level with the deck.
There, shamefaced, clumsy, pitiable,
He trails his grand white wings like oars.

A sailor mocks his limping gait
Or offers him a pipe to smoke.
The winged sky-wanderer, crippled now,
Has lost all dignity and state.

The poet in his cloud-dominions
Laughs at the fowler, rides the storm;
On earth amidst the jeers of men
Is maimed by his own giant pinions.

HARMONIES OF EVENING

[after *Harmonie du Soir* by Charles Baudelaire]

These are the moments when on vibrant stems
The flowers yield up their being like a censer.
Perfumes and sounds eddy upon the air
—A melancholy dance, a whirling languor.

The flowers yield up their being like a censer.
The violin shudders like a heart in torment
—A melancholy dance, a whirling languor.
The sky's sad beauty is a pilgrim's rest.

The violin shudders like a heart in torment,
A tender heart hating the black abyss.
The sky's sad beauty is a pilgrim's rest.
In its own stiffening blood the sun is drowned.

A tender heart hating the black abyss
Gathers all remnants of the luminous past.
In its own stiffening blood the sun is drowned.
Your memory glows within me like a chalice.

HUNTING HORNS

[after *Cors de Chasse* by Guillaume Apollinaire]

Noble and tragic as a tyrant's mask,
Our story has no drama and no peril.
No trivial touch lends pathos to our love.

Thomas de Quincey went to his poor Anne
In dreams of opium, poison sweet and chaste;
And since all passes, let us too pass by.
Let us pass by—but I shall turn again.

Our memories, are they not hunting horns,
Their resonances dying on the wind?

ALIENATION

[after *Vereinsamt* by Friedrich Nietsche]

Townwards on skirring wing
Now flies the raucous crow.
He has a home, and it is well with him;
Soon it will snow.

Stiff now you stand,
Backward your lingering gaze.

Fool—to have fled into the winter world
Before the bitter days.

The world that is a gate
Into a thousand waste-lands mute and cold
For one who has lost all you have lost
No resting-place can hold.

Now fated to a winter quest you stand
With terror in your eyes.
You are like smoke
For ever seeking colder skies.

Fly bird; grate out your song
With vulture voice.
Fool—let your bloody heart be hidden
By scorn and ice.

Townwards on skirring wing
Now flies the raucous crow;
Wretched is he who has no home—
Soon it will snow.

THE OFFICE DESK

[after *Aktentisch* by Theodor von Storm]

Today I signed directives at the office
And almost felt the common man's temptation
Of saying to myself 'A good day's work',
Deriving thence a stupid, small elation.

THE TWO

[after *Die Beiden* by Hugo von Hofmannsthal]

Like the full wine-cup in her hand
Her smiling mouth was round;
Her steadfast tread was light and sure,
No drop spilled on the ground.

The horse that carried him was young;
As firm as hers the hand
That with a careless movement made
His horse beside her stand.

But when he reached to take the cup,
Their fingers trembled so,
They saw between them on the ground
The red wine darkly flow.

WORLD'S END

[after *Weltende* by Jakob van Hoddis]

The hat flies off the bourgeois' pointed head.
The air is torn by screams on every side.
Slaters fall off the roofs and break in half.
On all sea coasts, we read, fast flows the tide.

Fast flows the tide. The tempest has arrived.
The wild waves hop ashore. The dams are
     crumbling.
Most of mankind are suffering from colds,
And from the bridges railway trains are tumbling.

POEM

[after *Gedicht* by Gottfried Benn]

And what do these compulsions mean,
Part word, part image and part notion?
From what internal pressure comes
This quiet, sorrowing emotion?

Impressions flow from nothingness,
From single things and from a heap.
One yields a flame, another ashes.
You scatter them, and quench, and keep.

Set frontiers, then, about some things:
You know you cannot grasp the whole.
Beneath the spell of vague misgivings
You will remain thus in control.

You shape and hammer and engrave
All day, all night, and Sundays too.
The vessel is of finished silver,
And it is being. It is you.

A DECLARATION OF LOVE

[after *Ein Liebes Bekenntnis* by Max Herrmann-
    Neisse]

To me your absence is like death;
My presence is like death to you.
I fail you: how can you forgive?
We kiss at parting—then alone we live.

And then alone you see my love.
In such a love where is the truth?
What use my sad and searching gaze
When never a spoken word my love betrays?

Once more you leave me here alone
Lost in a helpless agony
Which drives me out into the night . . .
My one desire to have you in my sight.

I hear the laughter in the houses;
I see the couples hurrying home
As if on wings, their arms entwined.
An envious fever suffocates my mind.

But if we were together now
Your eyes would not be on my book;
Shut and forbidding, I would see
Your loved face vainly beg one word from me.

So I demand perpetual pardon.
In debt to you until the end
I am your child: you gave me breath
And I require your blessing at my death.

AUTUMN TRANSFIGURED

[after *Verklärte Herbst* by Georg Trakl]

The closing year explodes
In golden wine and fruit;
The hushed woods standing round
Befriend the lonely man.

The labourer approves;
Birds greet him as he goes.
The soft, slow chimes of dusk
Give courage for the end.

It is love's gentle hour;
Image is one with image.
The blue stream bears the boat
In calm and silence down.

THE PLUM TREE

[after *Der Pflaumenbaum* by Bertold Brecht]

A puny tree grows in our yard—
A plum you'd hardly call it.
About this tree a paling stands
In case some harm befall it.

It can't grow big, though any tree
Would like the chance to sprout;
But that can never happen here:
The sun is quite shut out.

You wouldn't know it was a plum;
It's never borne a fruit.
Yet you can tell what tree it is
In spring when green leaves shoot.

Uncollected

THE SPECIAL DAY

Cooling your eyes upon the special day,
You let the fever burn itself away.

The weeds proliferate like private problems.
You tear them out; they multiply fourfold.
So it is now; so it will always be.

But rest your hearing on soft foreign voices.
Arrange your face between your hands and stare:
Cooling your eyes upon the special day,
You let the fever burn itself away.

MADONNA FACES

Madonna faces in the brain remain.
Then, as the months revolve
Like centuries' corruption of a fresco,
Madonna faces in the brain dissolve.
They leave a stain.
And whether there is loss or gain
Is what the incessant brain
Desires to be assured,
Demands in vain.

Ponder the mural blank, the cancelled faces,
The delectation of compulsive pain.

Unpublished

Index of Titles
and First Lines

176

179